Eugene Delacroix: 150 Masterpieces

By Maria Tsaneva

First Edition

*****

I0477285

Eugene Delacroix: 150 Masterpieces
*****

Foreword

Eugene Delacroix was the greatest French painter of the Romantic Movement. He was the son of a politician, Charles Delacroix, but there is some evidence to indicate that his real father was the diplomat Talleyrand, a friend of the family. His mother, Victoire Oeben, came of a family of notable craftsmen and designers.

In 1816 Delacroix entered the studio of Pierre Guerin, who had earlier taught Gericault. His basic artistic education was obtained, however, by copying Old Masters at the Louvre, where he delighted in Rubens and the Venetian School. He met Bonington in the Louvre and was introduced by him to English watercolour painting. Constable's Hay Wain, exhibited in the 1824 Salon, also made a great impression on him and in 1825 he spent some months in England, admiring in particular Gainsborough, Lawrence, Etty, and Wilkie. In the Salon of 1822 he had his first public success with The Barque of Dante (Louvre, Paris). It was bought by the State, as was The Massacre at Chios (Louvre) two years later, ensuring the success of his career. Gros called this painting 'the massacre of painting', but Baudelaire wrote that it was a terrifying hymn in honour of doom and irremediable suffering.

In 1832 Delacroix visited Morocco in the entourage of the Comte de Mornay and there acquired a fund of rich and exotic visual imagery which he exploited to the full in his later work (Sultan of Morocco, 1845). From the late 1830s his style and technique underwent a change. In place of luminous glazes and contrasted values he began to use a personal technique of vibrating adjacent tones and colour effects in a manner of which Watteau had been a master, making colour enter into the structure of the picture to an extent which had not previously been attempted. In spite of being hailed as the leader of the Romantic Movement, his predilection for exotic and emotionally charged subject-matter, and his open enmity with Ingres, Delacroix always claimed allegiance to the classical tradition and for his large works followed the traditional course of making numerous preparatory drawings.

In his later career he became one of the most distinguished monumental mural painters in the history of French art. His public commissions included decorations in several major buildings in Paris: Palais Bourbon (Salon du roi); of the Luxembourg Palace (1841-46); and three paintings in the Chapelle des Anges of S. Sulpice (1853-61). In the last of these, his Jacob and the Angel and Heliodorus Expelled from the Temple are among the maturest expressions of his decorative richness of colour and grandiose structural integration. Baudelaire said of him that he was the only artist who 'in our faithless generation conceived religious pictures' and van Gogh wrote: 'Only Rembrandt and Delacroix could paint the face of Christ.'

Delacroix's output was enormous. After his death his executors found more than 9,000 paintings, pastels, and drawings in his studio and he prided himself on the speed at which he worked, declaring 'If you are not skilful enough to sketch a man falling out of a window during the time it takes him to get from the fifth storey to the ground, then you will never be able to produce monumental work.' Among great painters he was also one of the finest writers on art. He was a voluminous letter writer and kept a journal from 1822 to 1824 and again from 1847 until his death - a marvellously rich source of information and opinion on his life and times. His influence, particularly through his use of colour, was prodigious, inspiring Renoir, Seurat, and van Gogh among others. Delacroix's studio in Paris is now a museum devoted to his life and work, but the Louvre has the finest collection of his paintings.

Paintings and Drawings

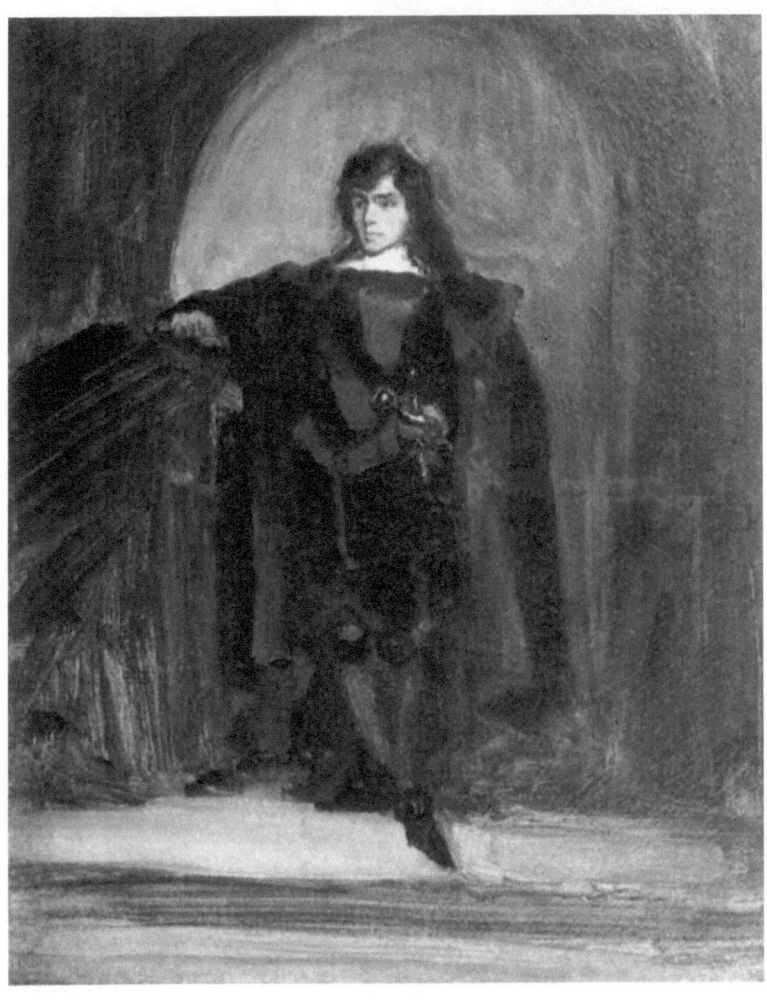

Self Portrait as Hamlet, 1821
Oil on canvas

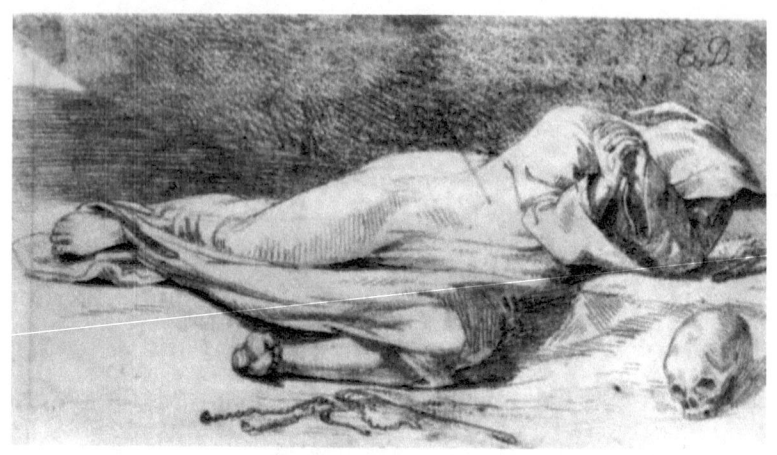

Monk at Prayer, 1821
Graphite

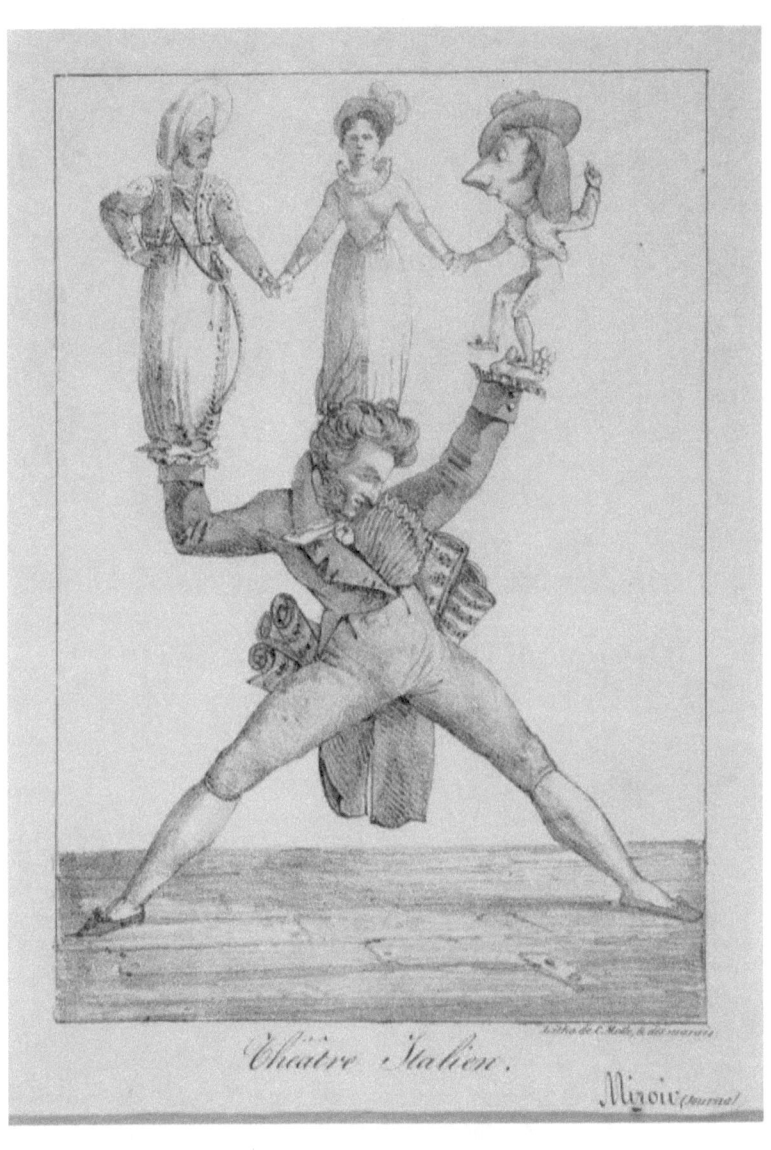

The Italian Theatre, 1821
Lithography

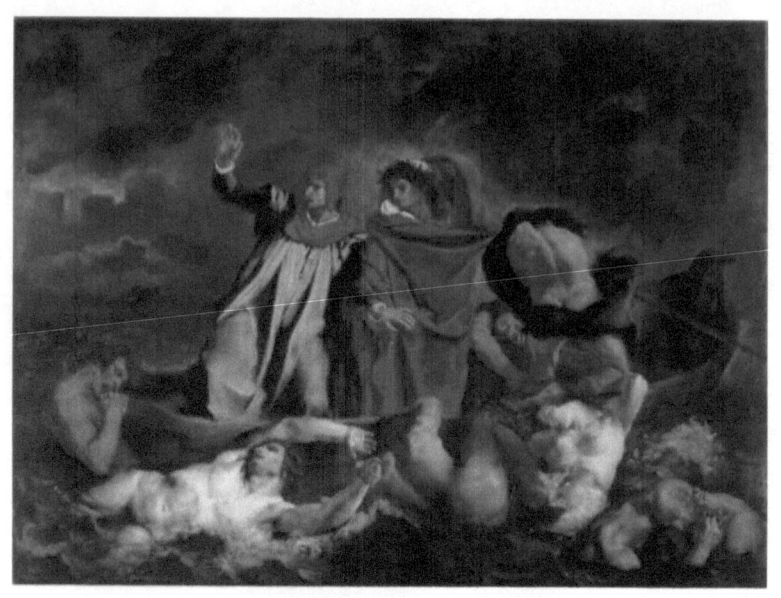

The Barque of Dante (Dante and Virgil in the
Underworld), 1822
Oil on canvas

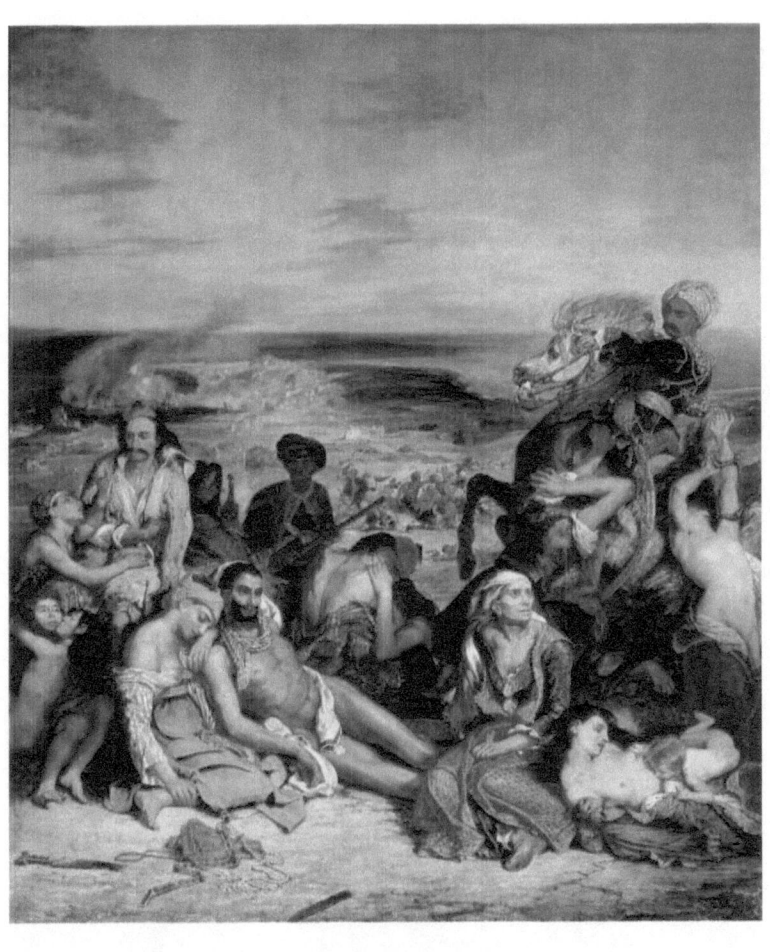

Scenes from the Massacre of Chios, 1822
Oil on canvas

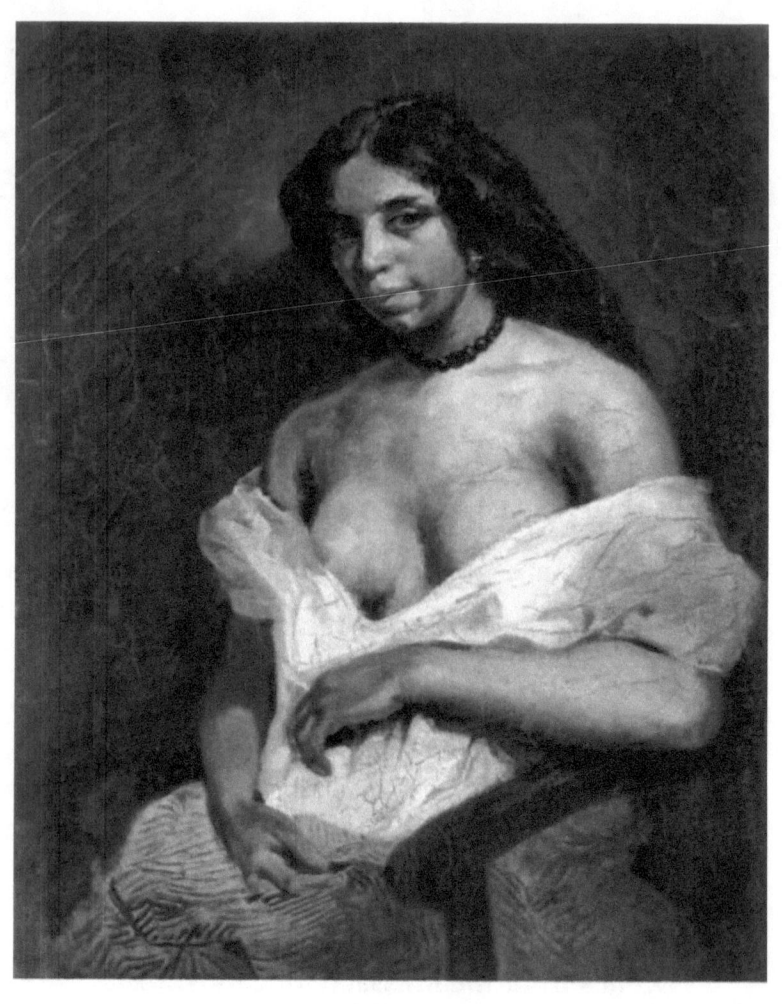

A Mulatto Woman, c.1821-c.1824
Oil on canvas

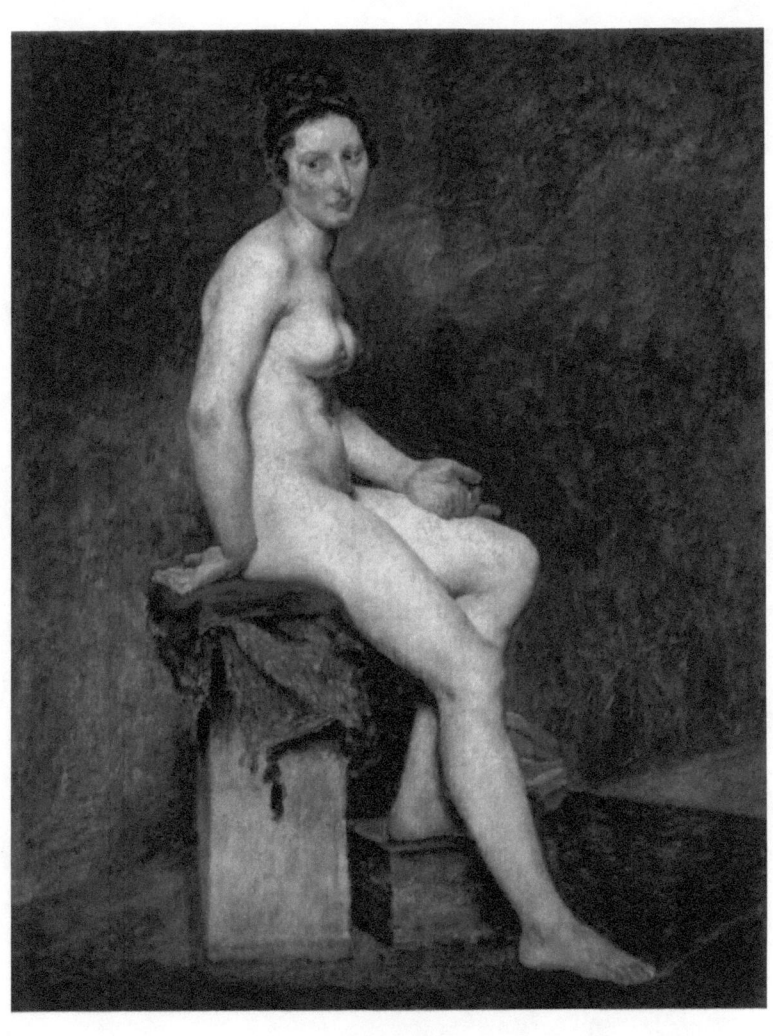

Seated Nude, Mademoiselle Rose, 1820-1824
Oil on canvas

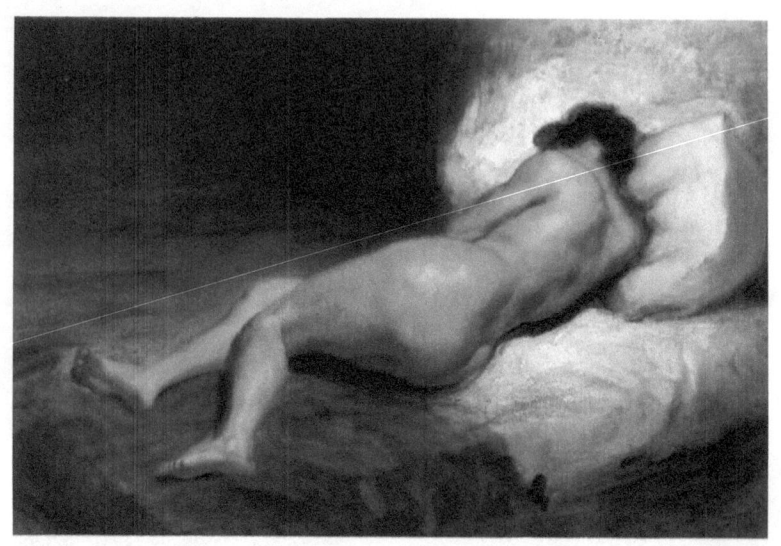

Study of a Reclining Nude, 1824
Oil on canvas

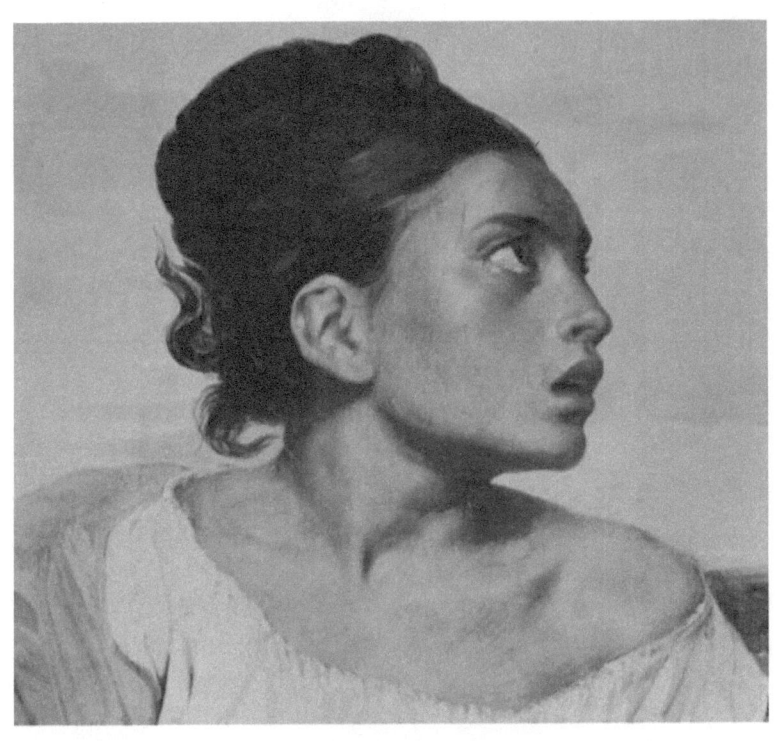

The Orphan Girl at the Cemetery, 1823-1824
Oil on canvas

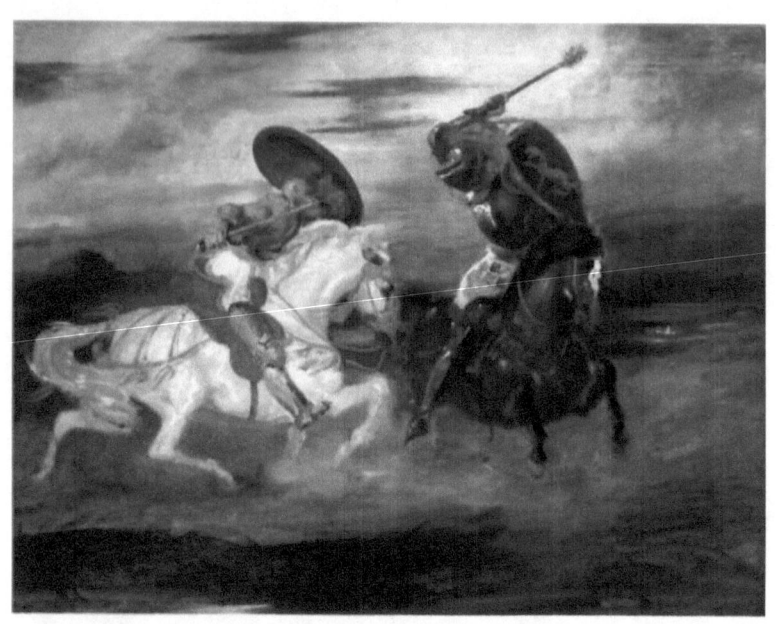

Two Knights Fighting in a Landscape, c.1824
Oil on canvas

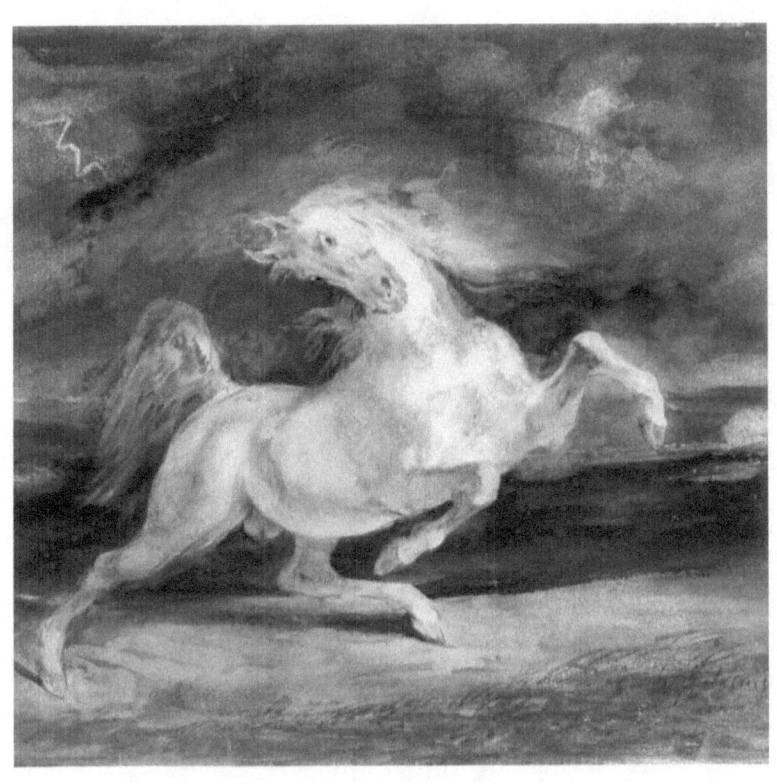

Horse Frightened by a Storm, 1824
Watercolour

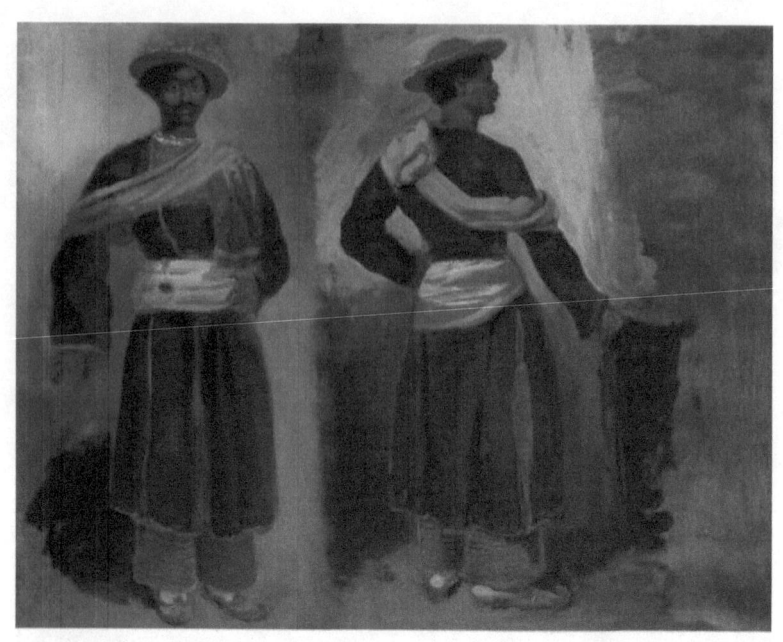

Two Views of a Standing Indian from Calcutta, 1823-
1824
Oil on canvas

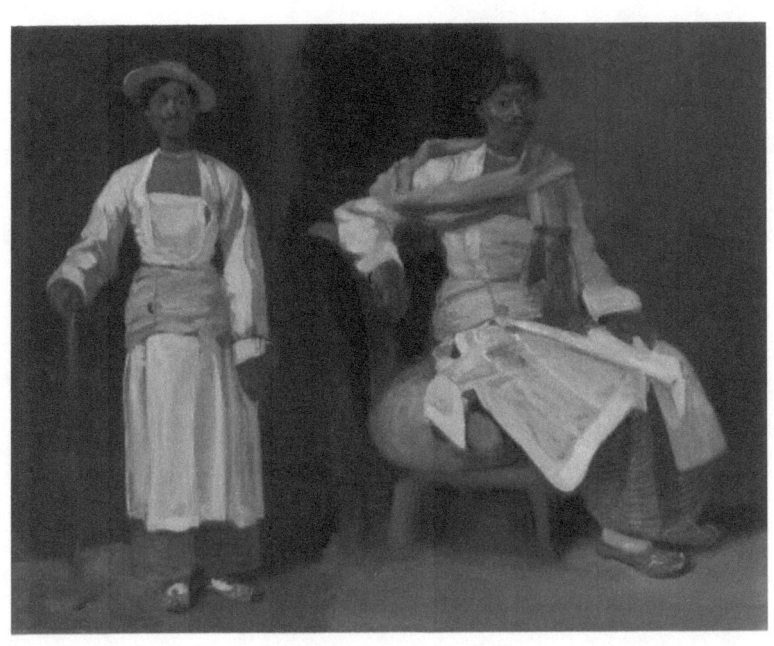

Two Views of an Indian from Calcutta, Seated and
Standing, 1823-1824
Oil on canvas

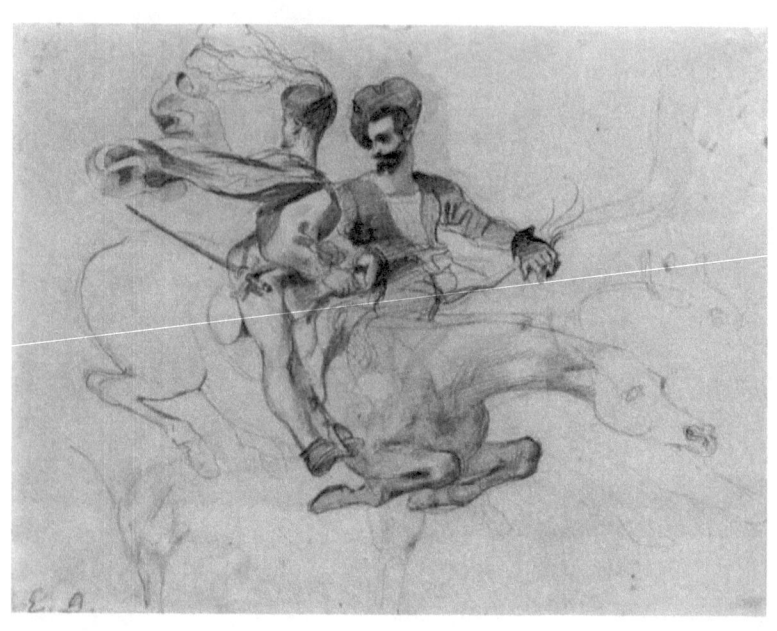

Illustration for Goethe's Faust, 1825-27
Pencil on beige paper

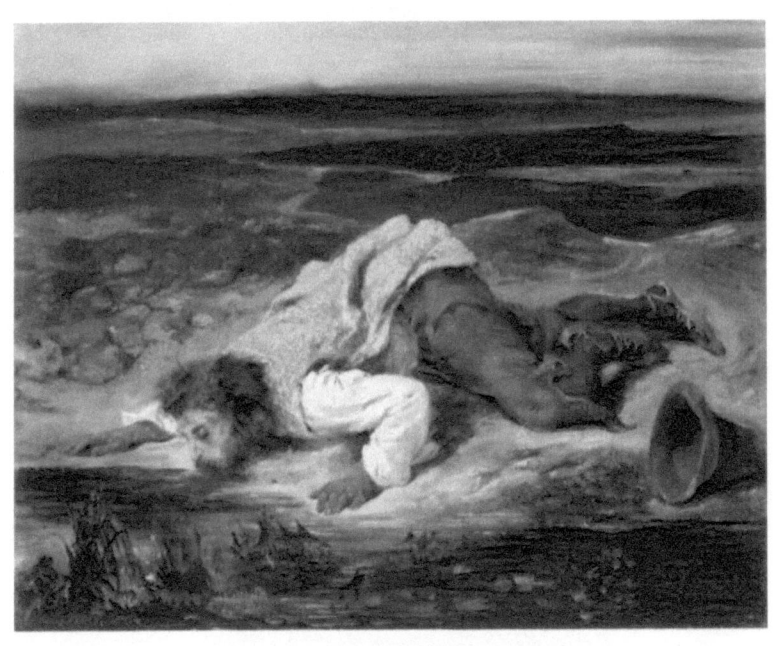

A Mortally Wounded Brigand Quenches his Thirst,
1825
Oil on canvas

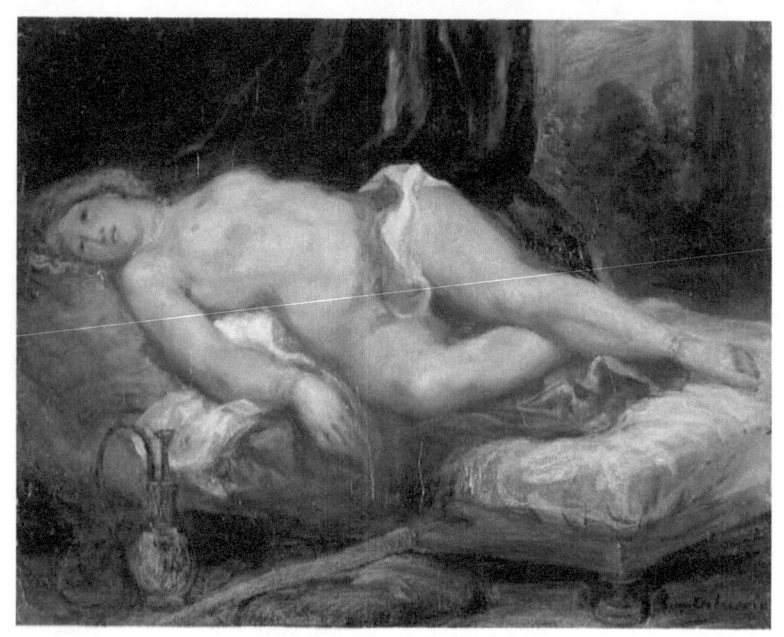

Odalisque, c.1825
Oil on canvas

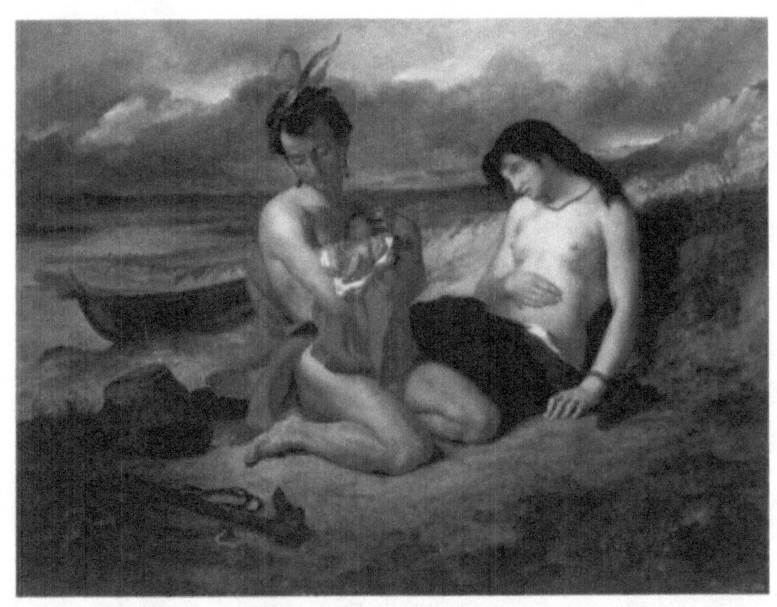

The Natchez, 1823-1825
Oil on canvas

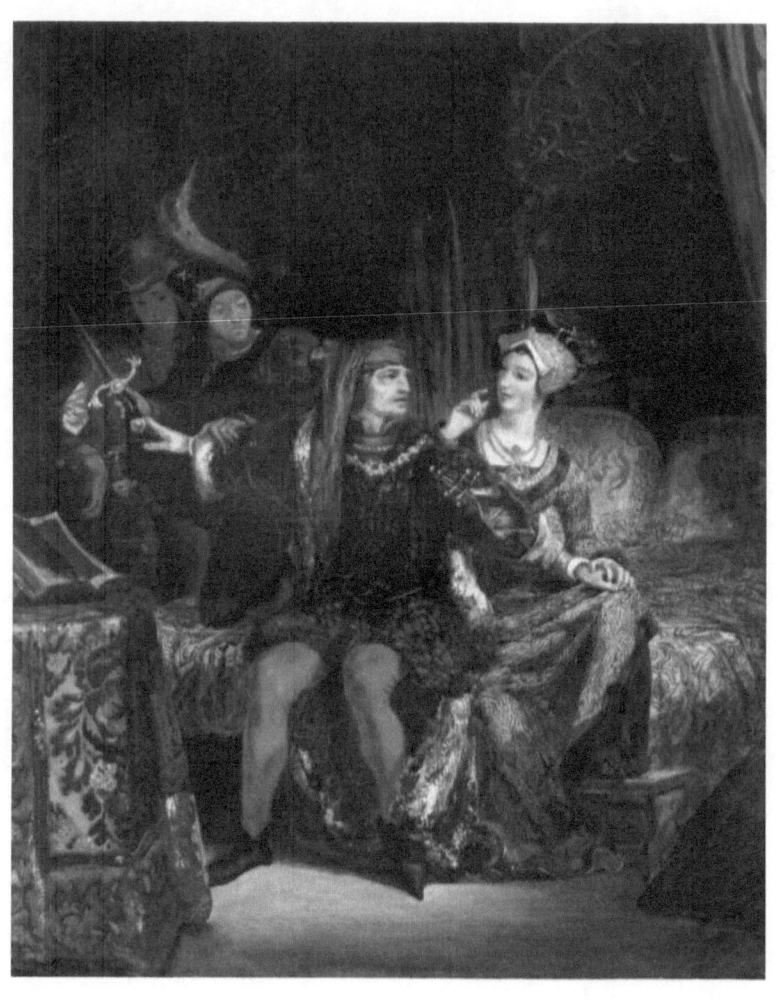

Charles VI and Odette de Champdivers, 1824-1826
Oil on canvas

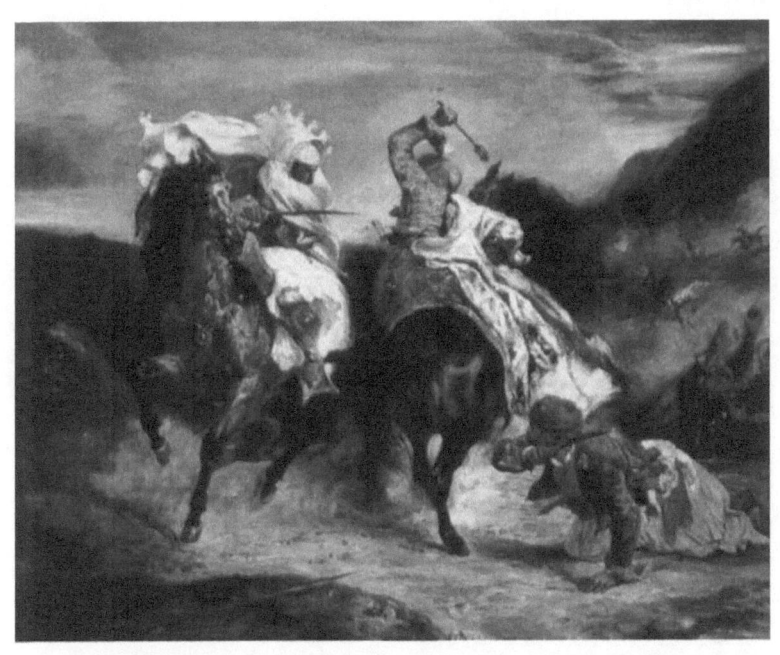

Combat Between the Giaour and the Pasha, 1826
Oil on canvas

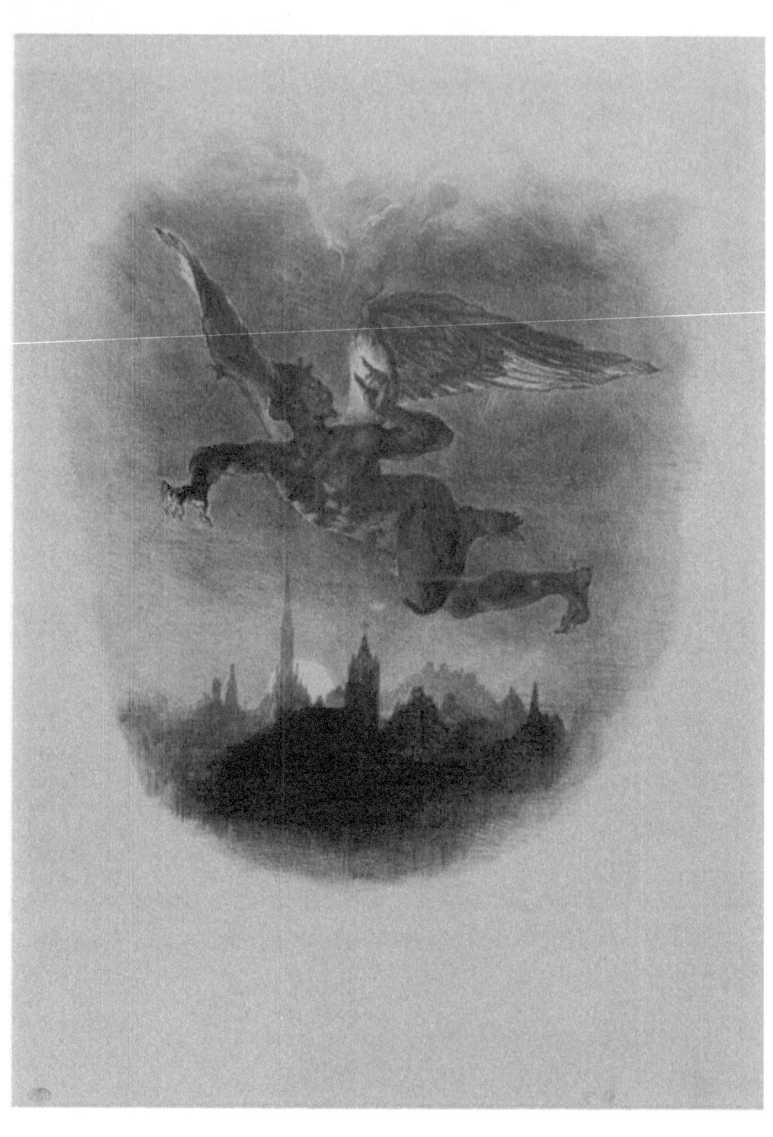

Mephistopheles Aloft, 1826
Lithography

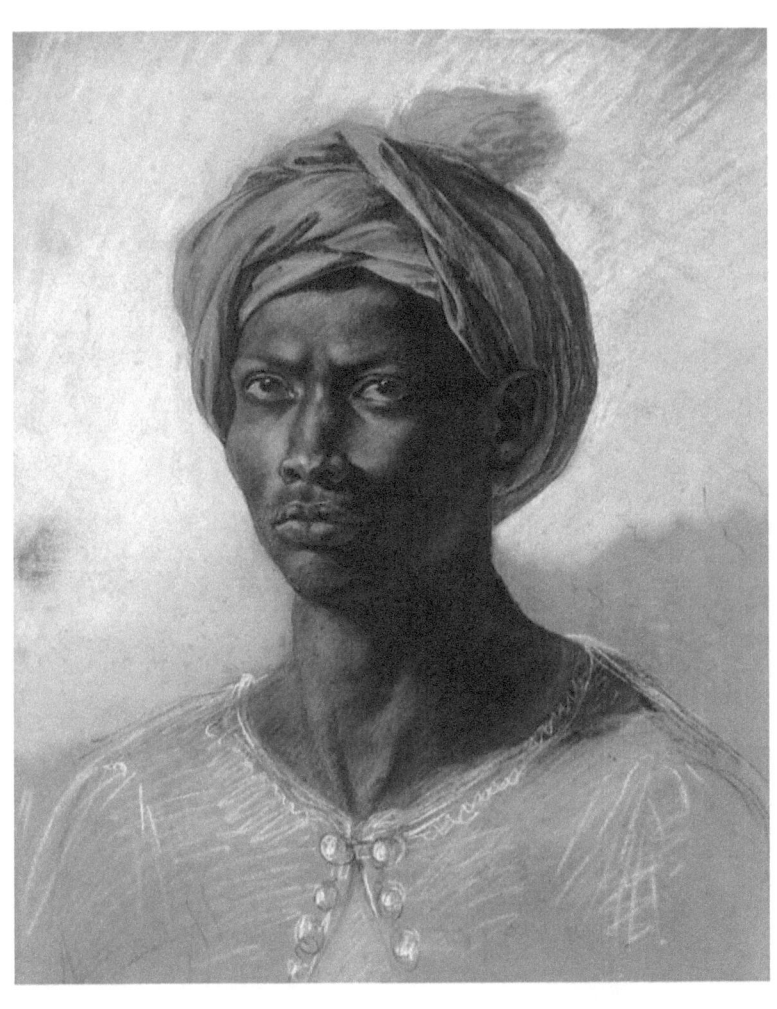

Portrait of a Turk in a Turban, 1826
Pastel

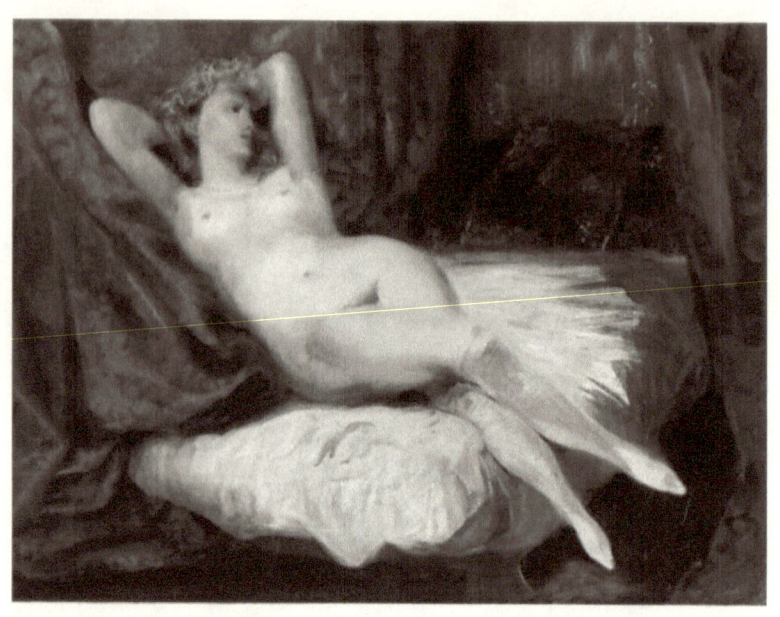

Female Nude Reclining on a Divan, 1825-1826
Oil on canvas

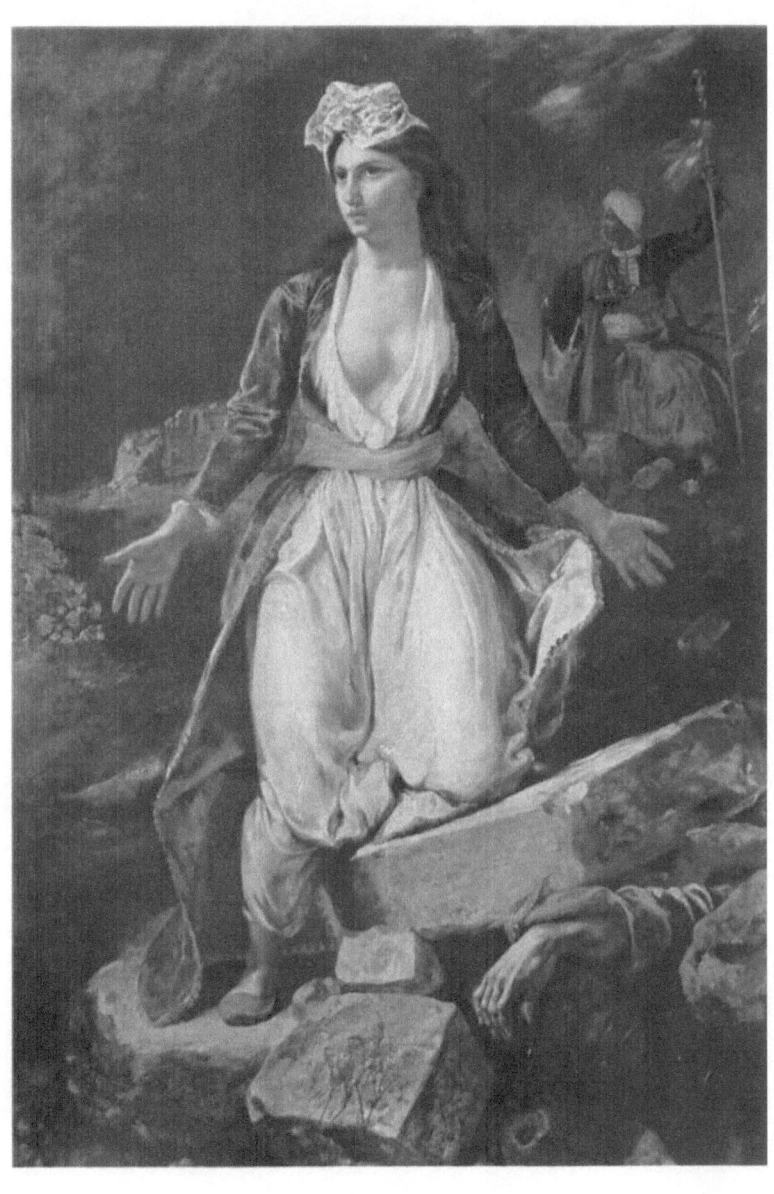

Greece expiring on the Ruins of Missolonghi, 1826
Oil on canvas

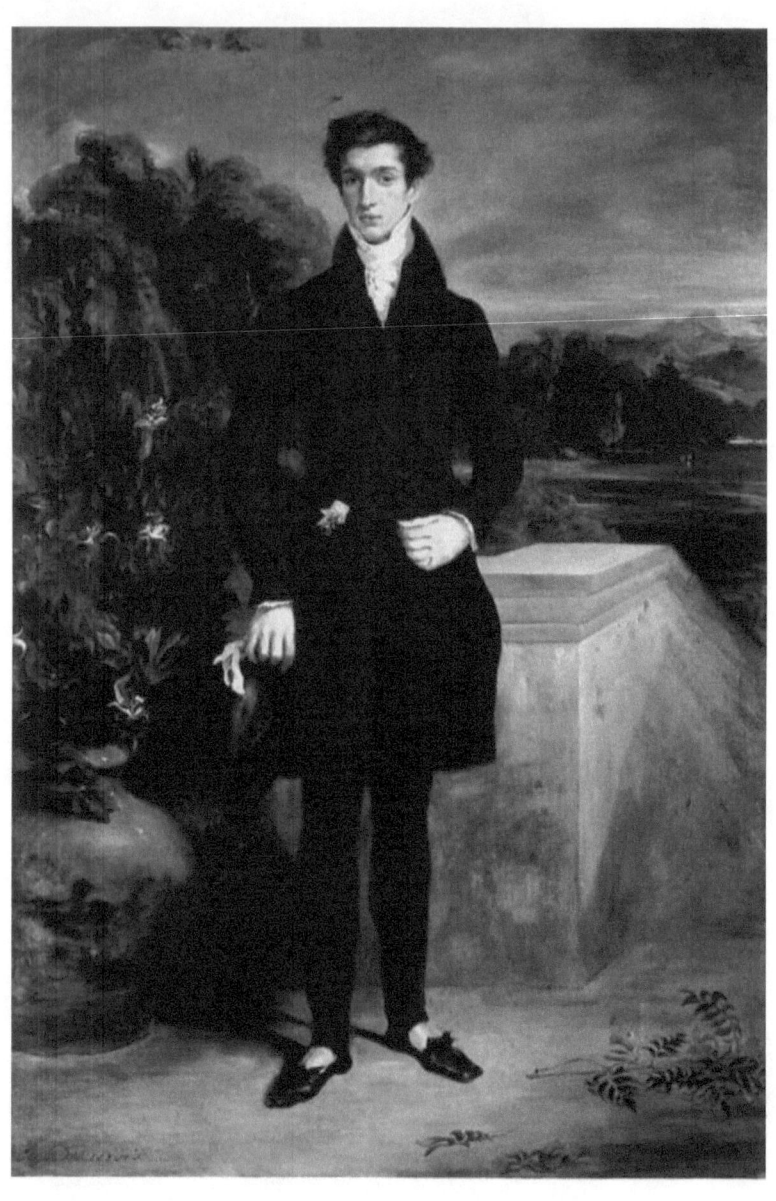

Portrait of Baron Schwiter, 1827
Oil on canvas

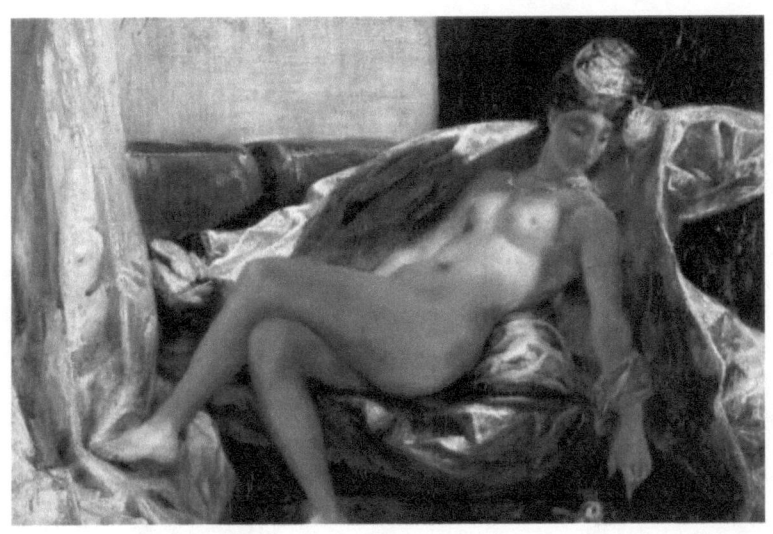

Reclining Odalisque or, Woman with a Parakeet, 1827
Oil on canvas

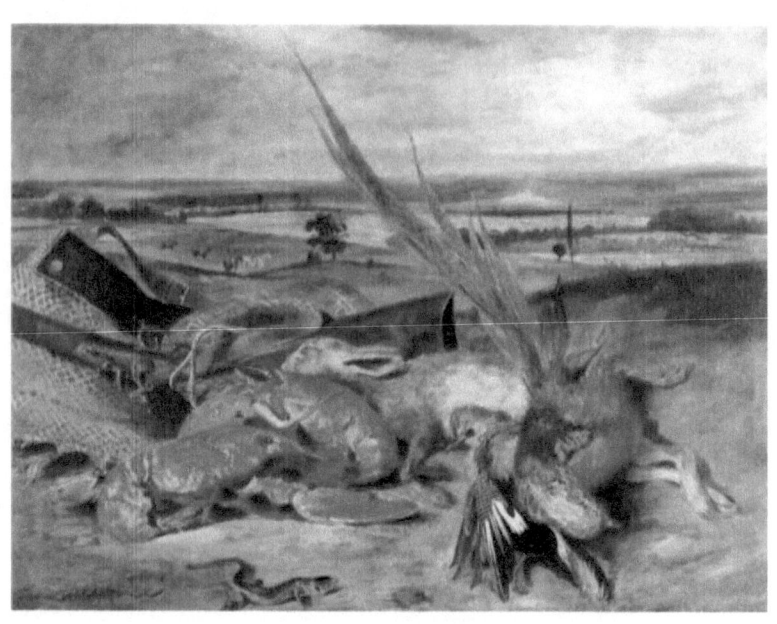

Still Life with Lobsters, 1826-1827
Oil on canvas

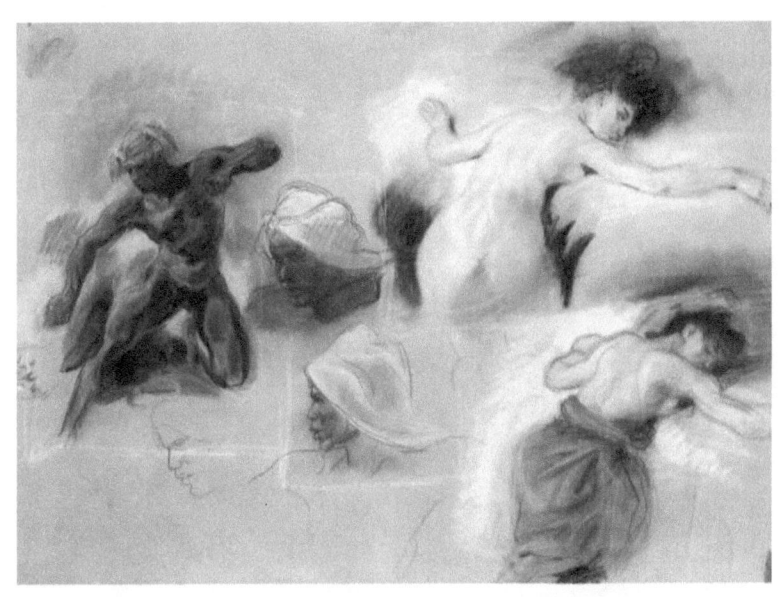

Sketch for The Death of Sardanapalus, 1827

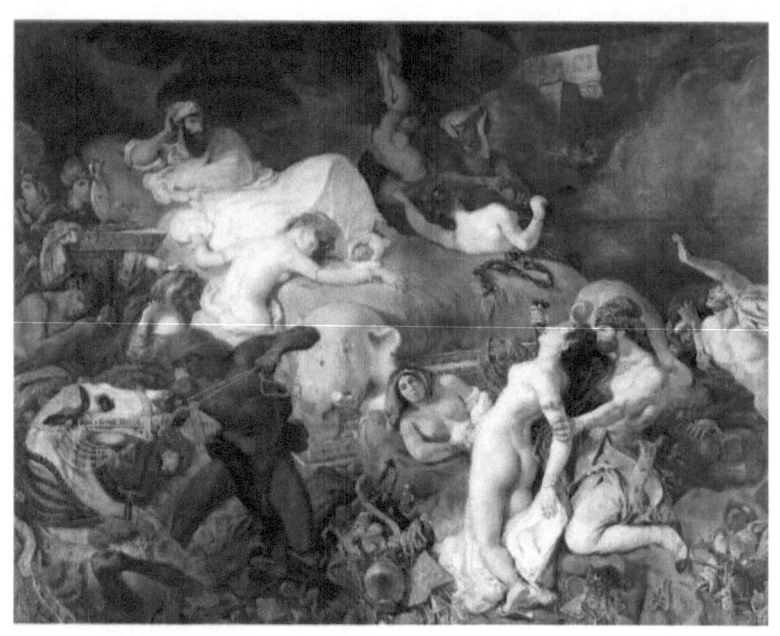

Death of Sardanapalus, 1827
Oil on canvas

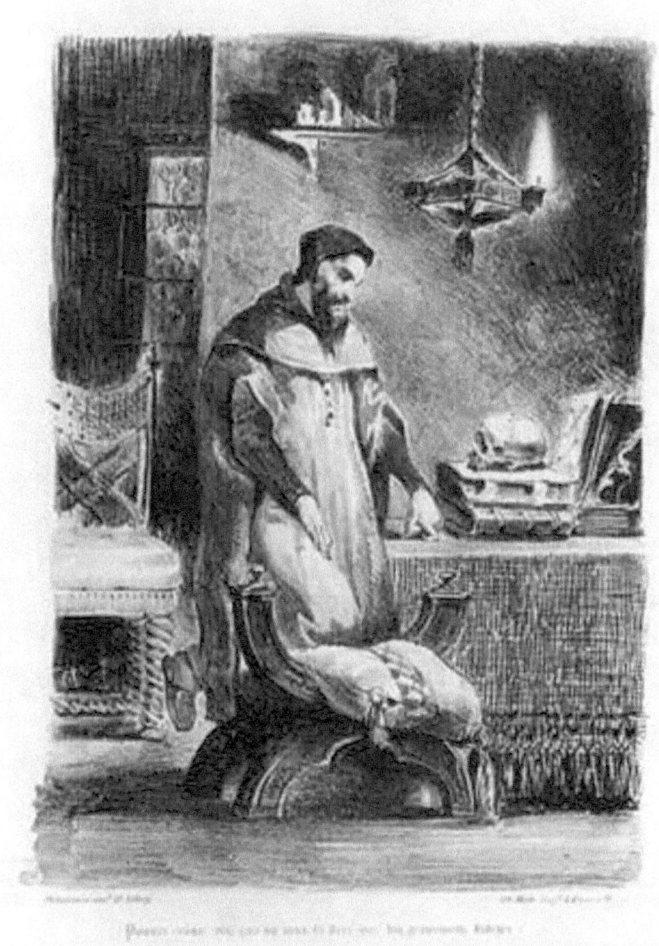

Faust in his Study, 1828
Lithography

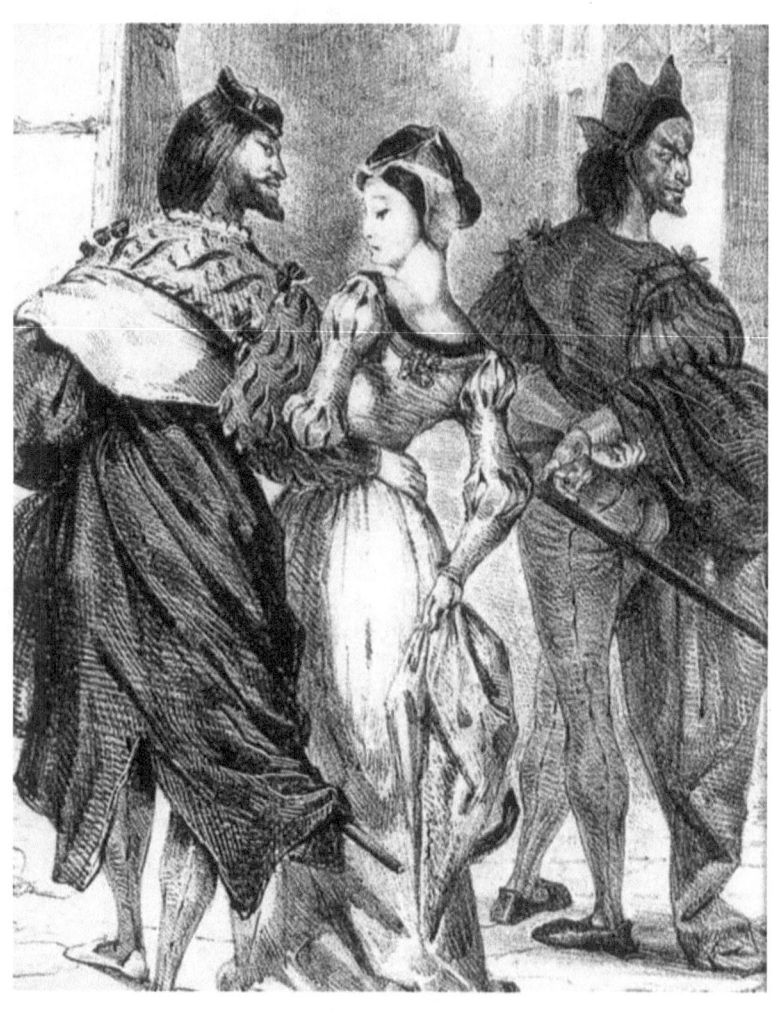

Faust meeting Marguerite, 1828
Lithography

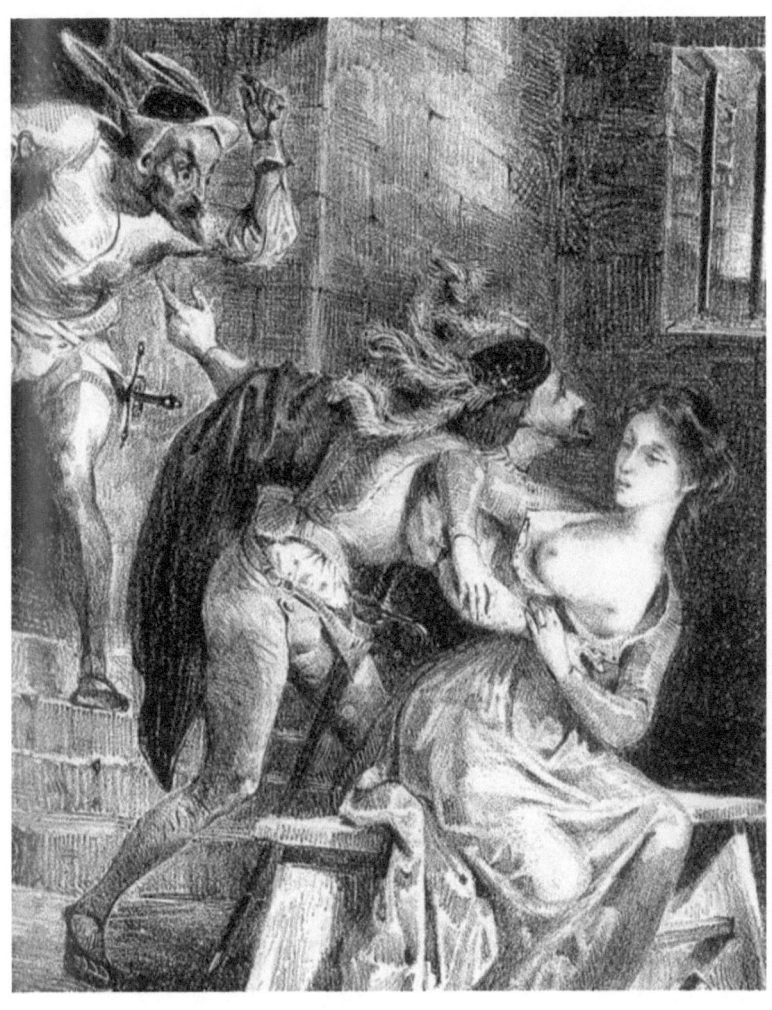

Faust rescues Marguerite from her prison, 1828
Lithography

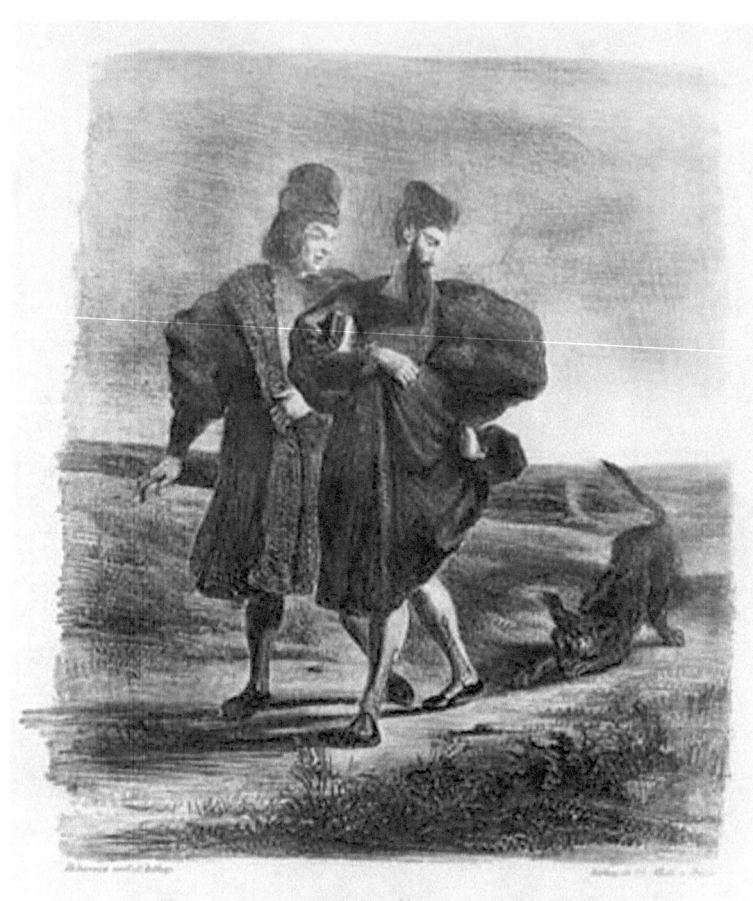

Faust, Goethe's Tragedy, 1828
Lithography

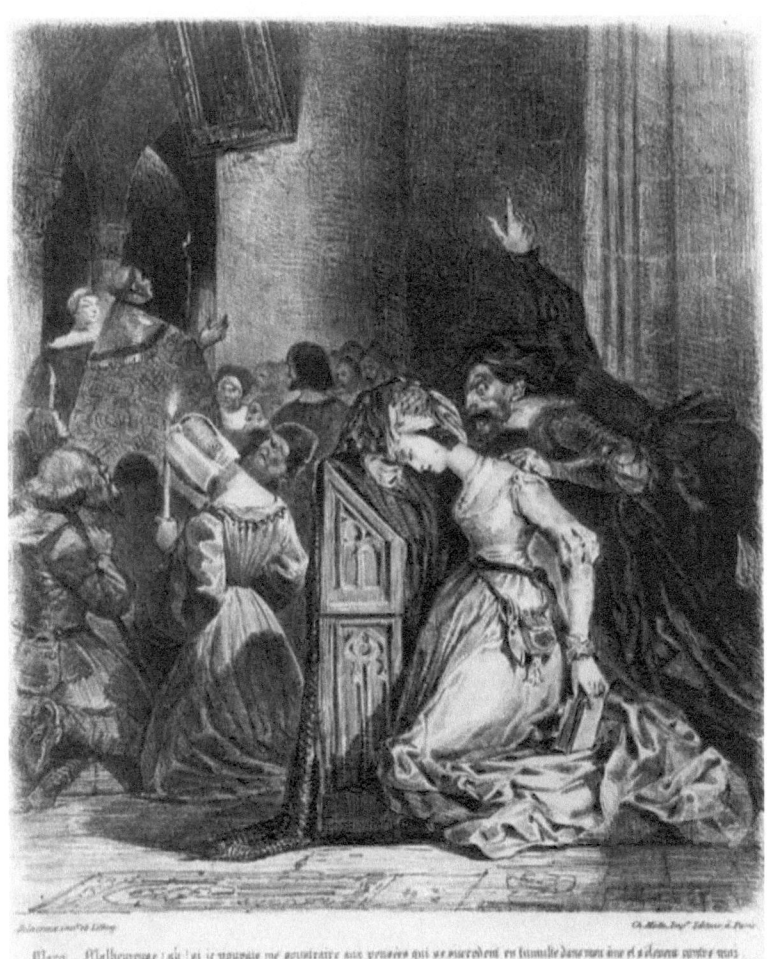

Marguerite in the Church with the Evil Spirits, 1828
Lithography

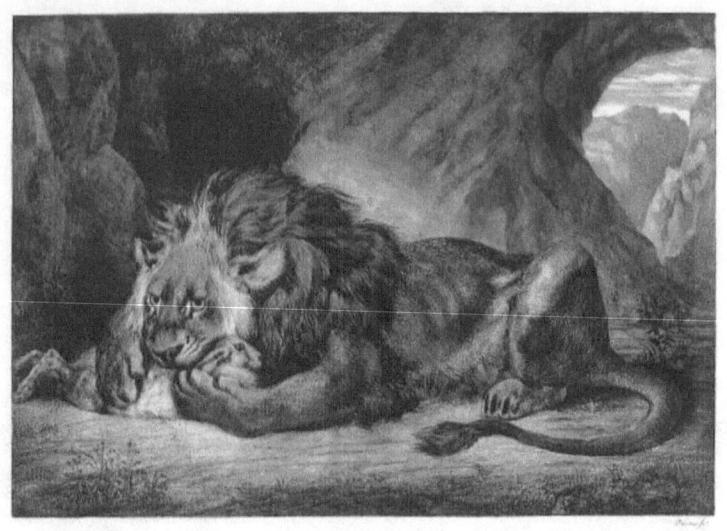

Lion of the Atlas, 1829
Lithography

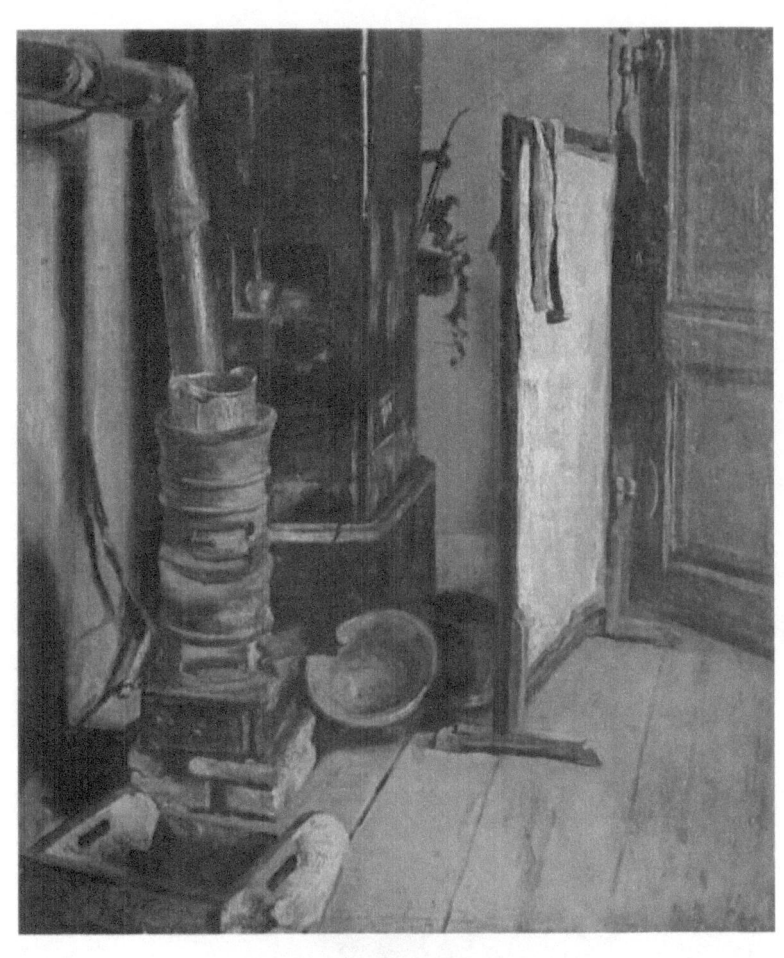

A corner of the studio, c.1830
Oil on canvas

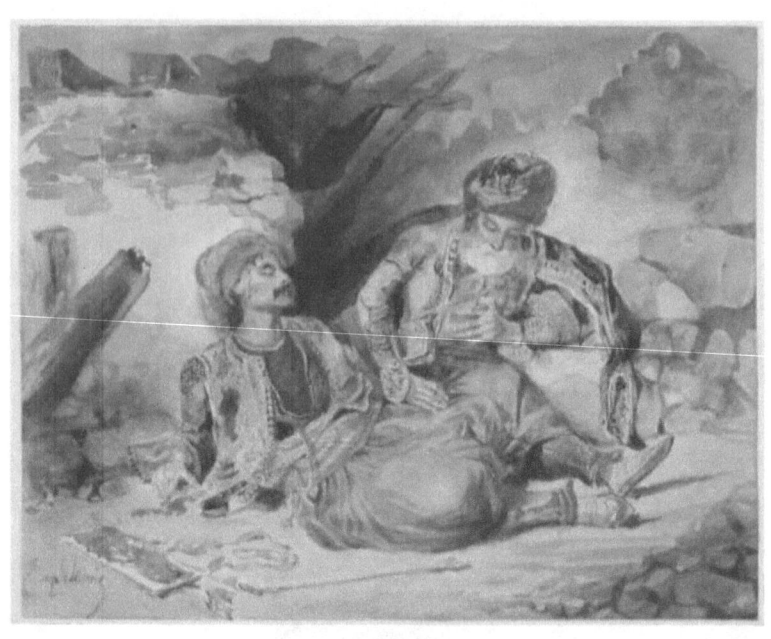

The Dying Turk, 1825-1830
Watercolor

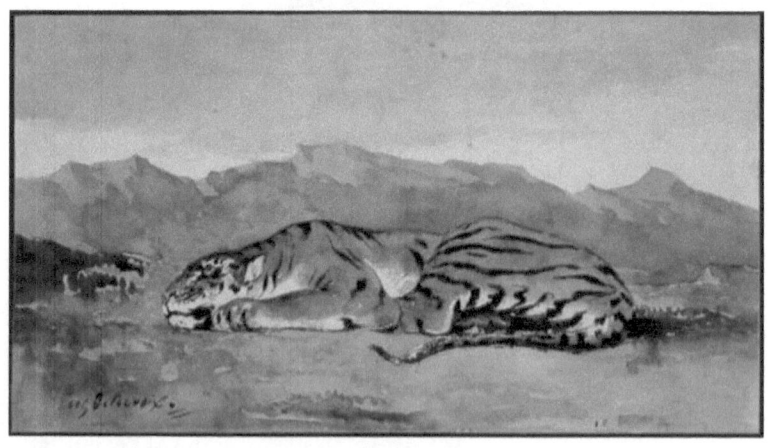

Tiger, 1830
Watercolor

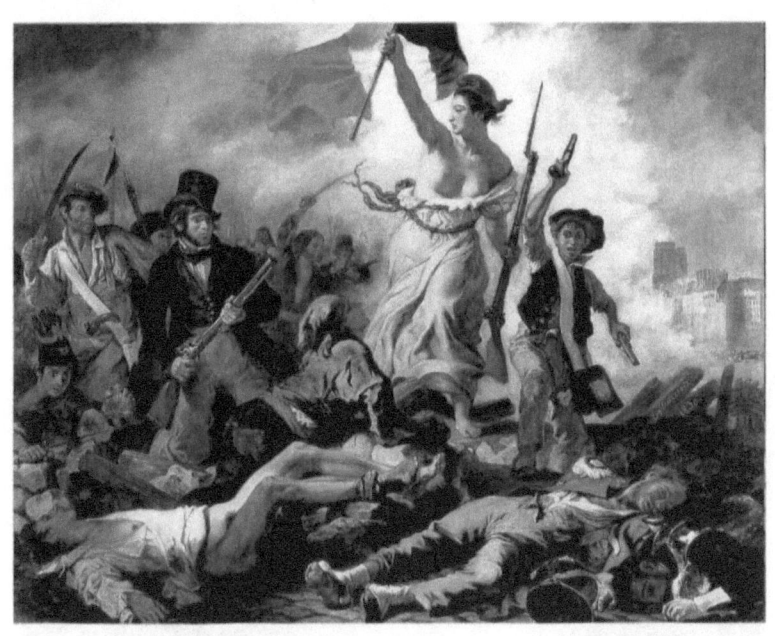

The Liberty Leading the People, 1830
Oil on canvas

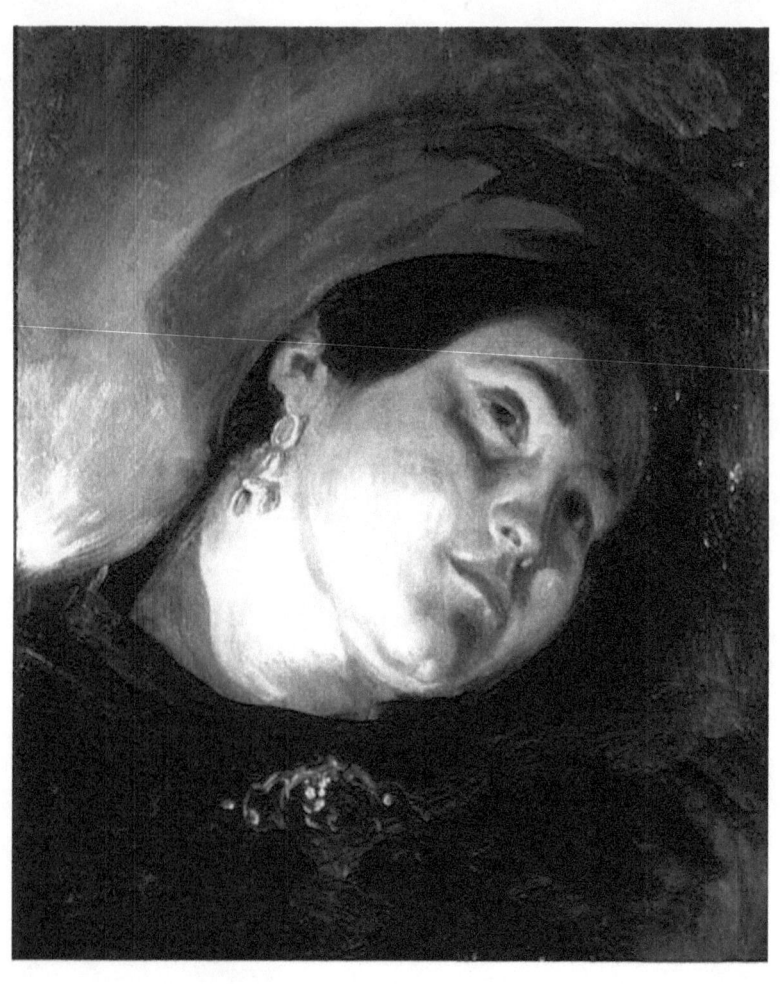

Head of a Woman in a Red Turban, 1831
Oil

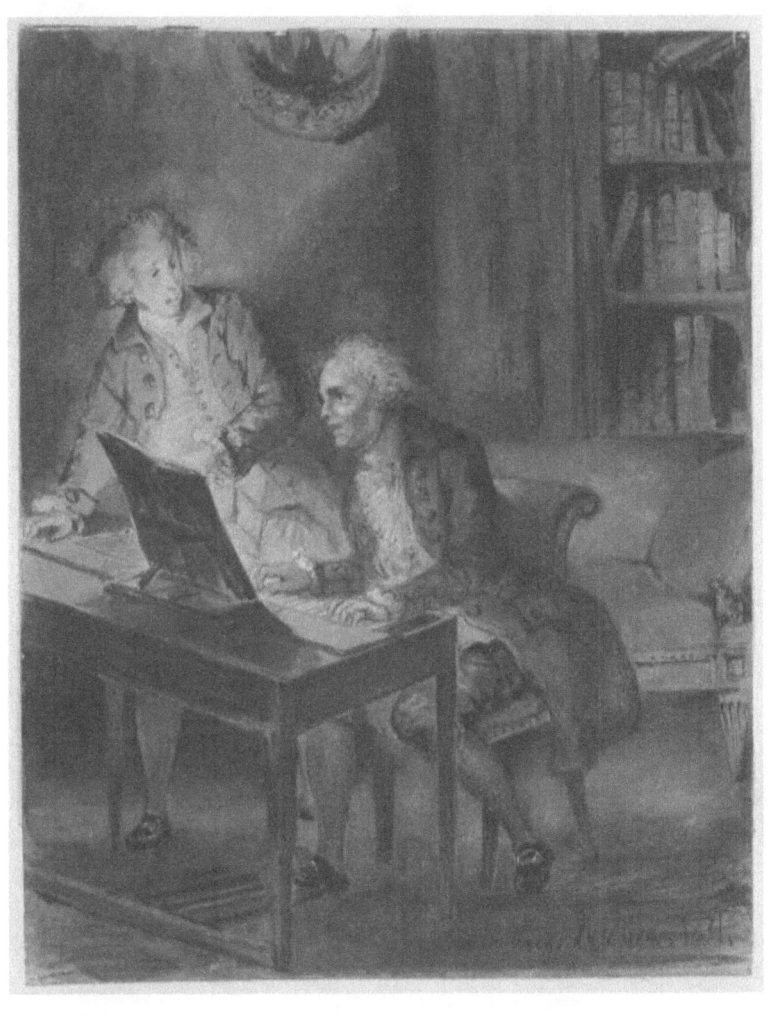

Willibald von Glueck at the Clavecin Composing the
Score of his Armide, 1831
Watercolor

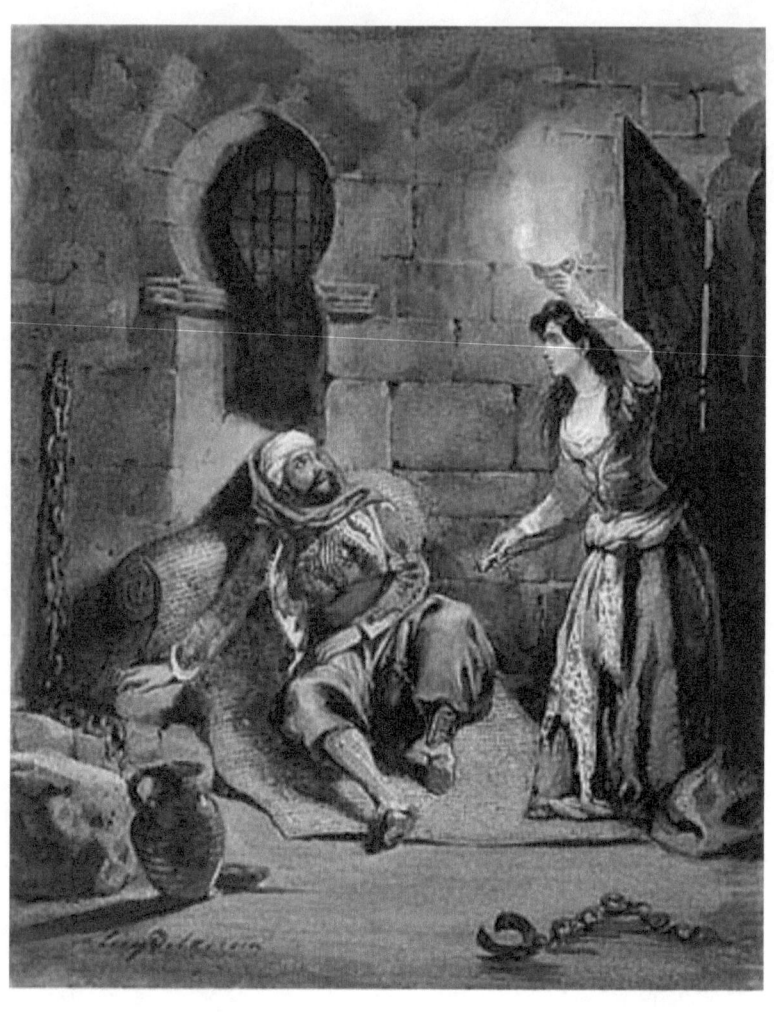

Episode from The Corsair by Lord Byron, 1831
Gouache, graphite, ink, watercolor

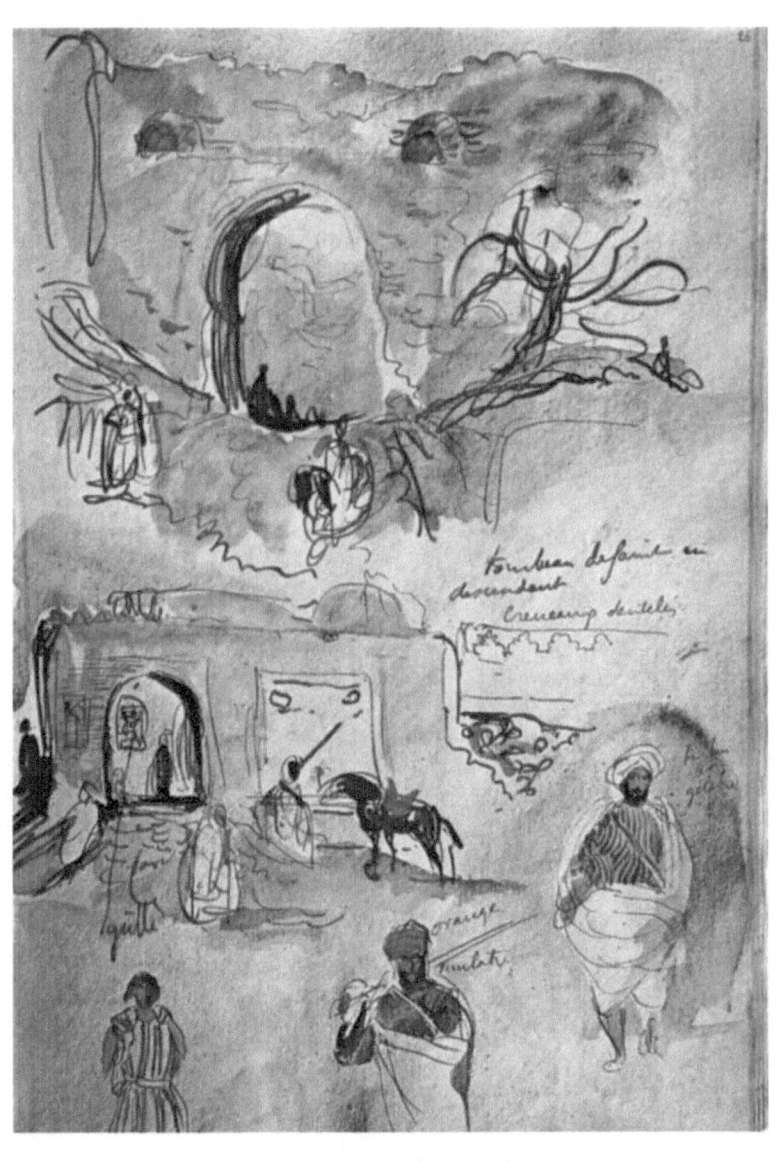

City wall of Meknes (Morocco from the sketchbook),
1832
Pencil, pen, tusche

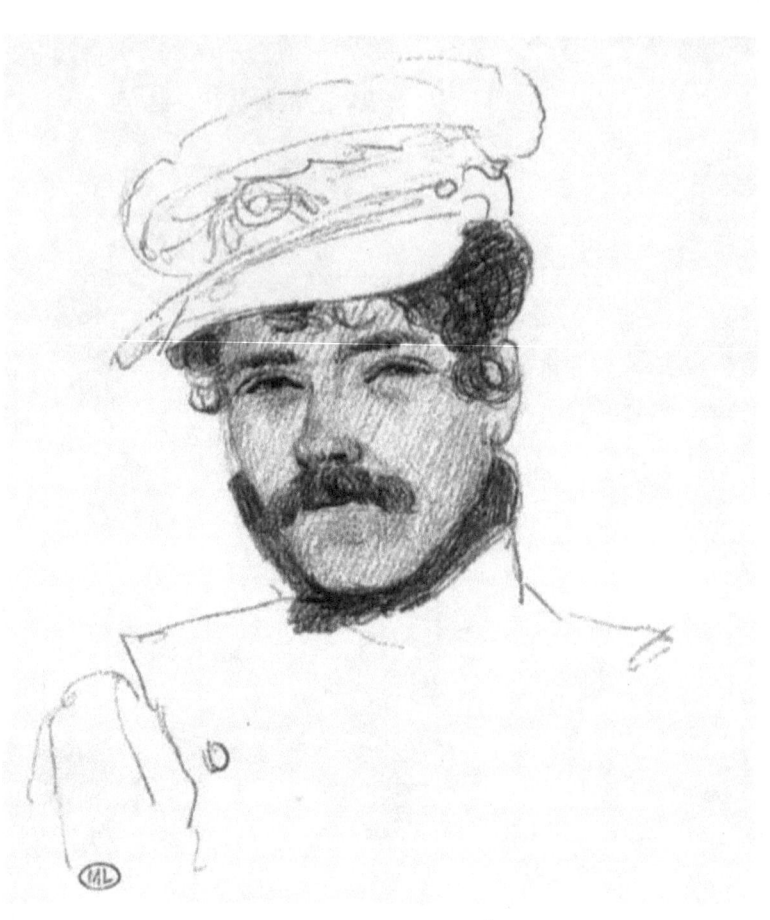

Self-Portrait with Cap, 1832
Drawing

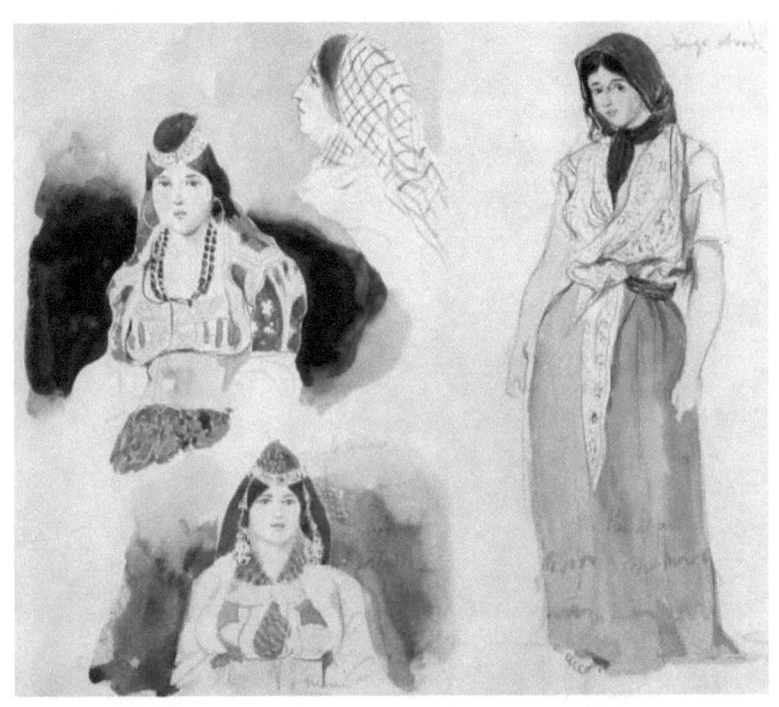

Moroccan Women, 1832
Watercolor

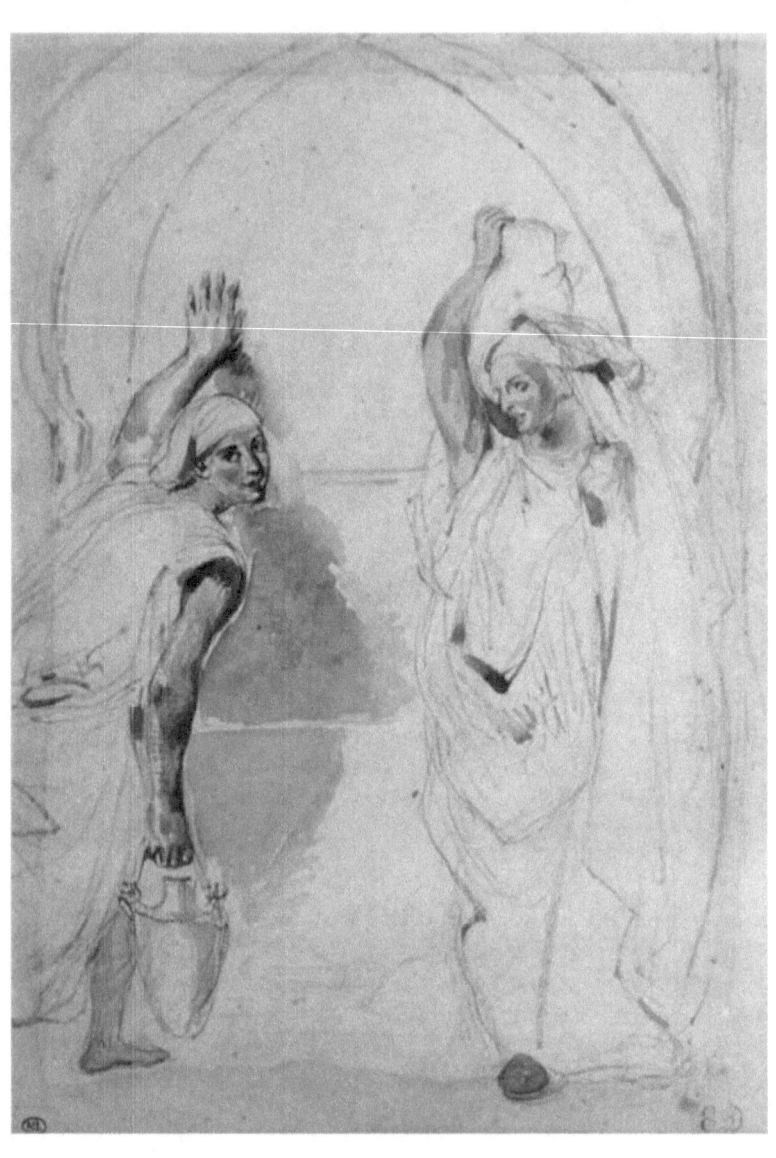

Two Women at the Well, 1832
Watercolor

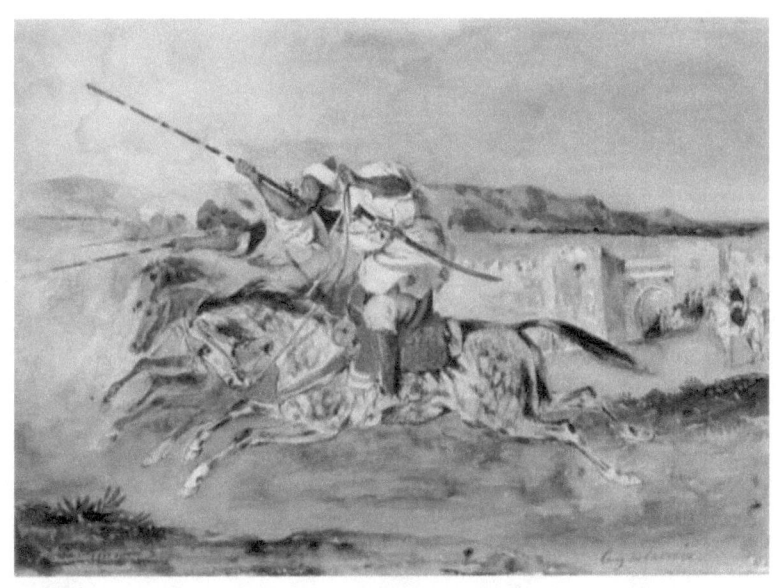

Arab Fantasia, 1832
Watercolor

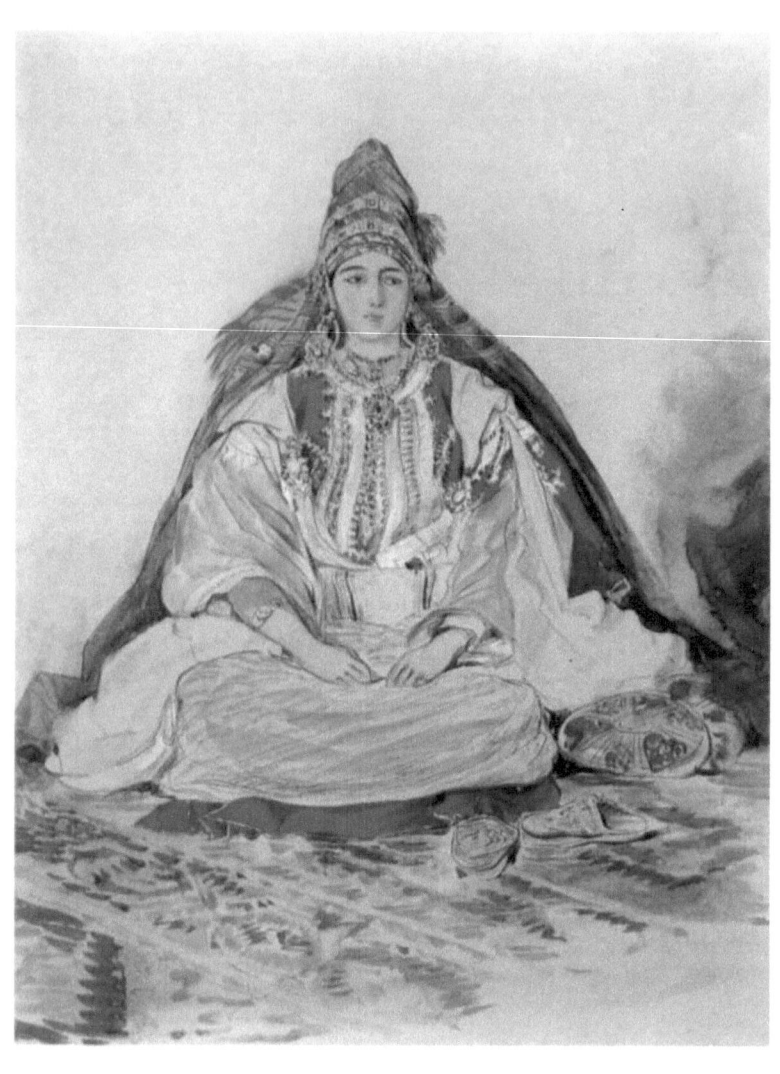

Jewish Bride, 1832
Watercolor

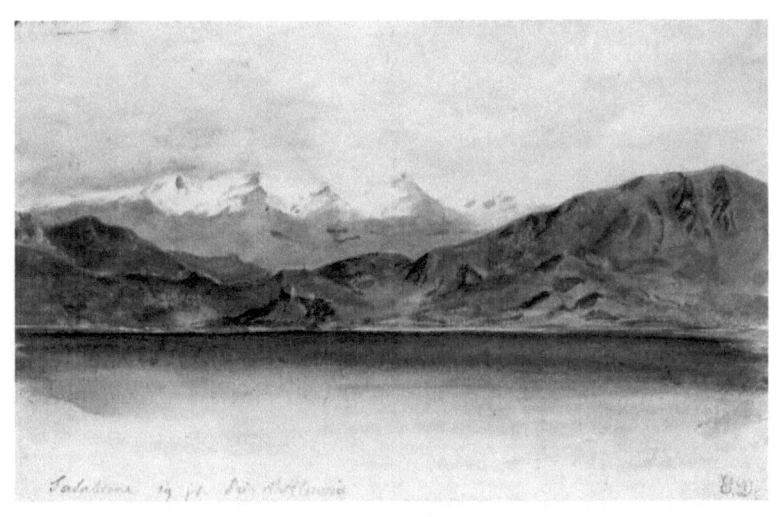

The Coast of Spain at Salabrena, 1832
Watercolor

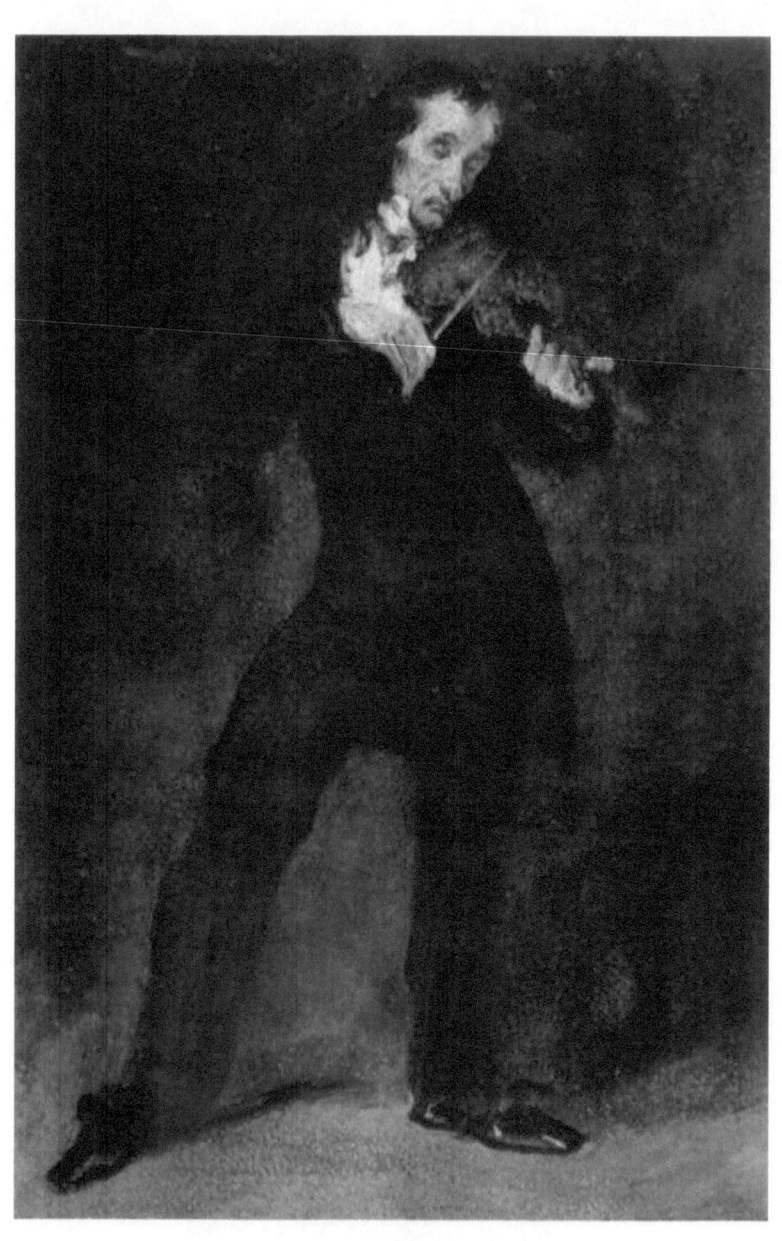

Portrait of Paganini, 1832
Oil on canvas

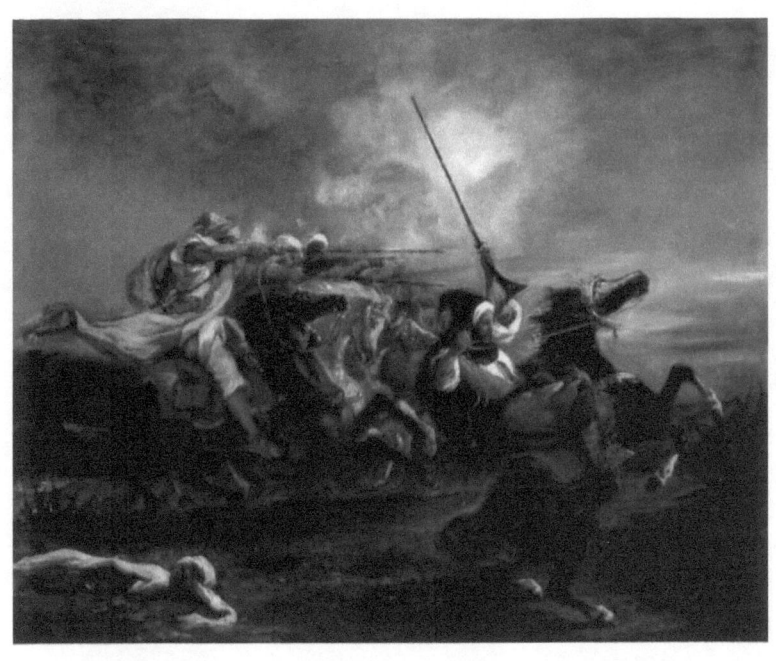

Moroccan horsemen in military action, 1832
Oil on canvas

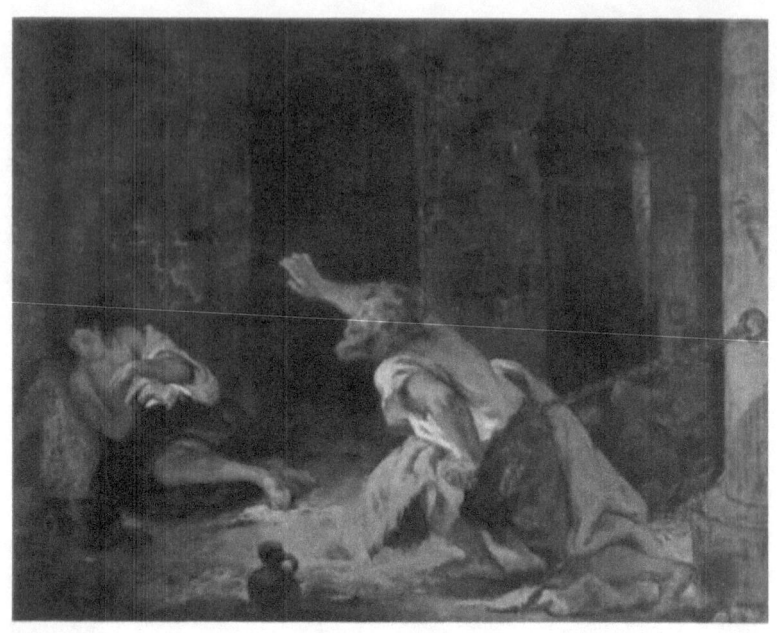

The Prisoner of Chillon, 1834
Oil on canvas

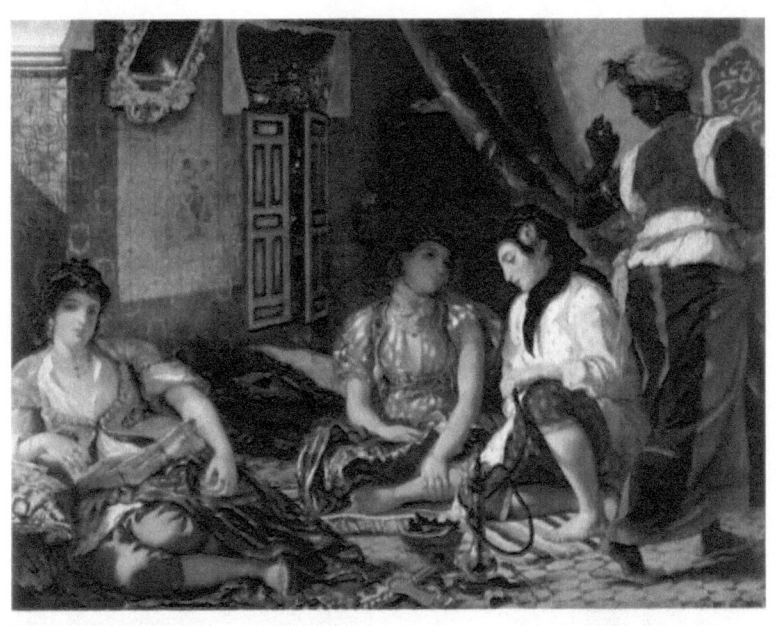

The Women of Algiers in their Apartment, 1834
Oil on canvas

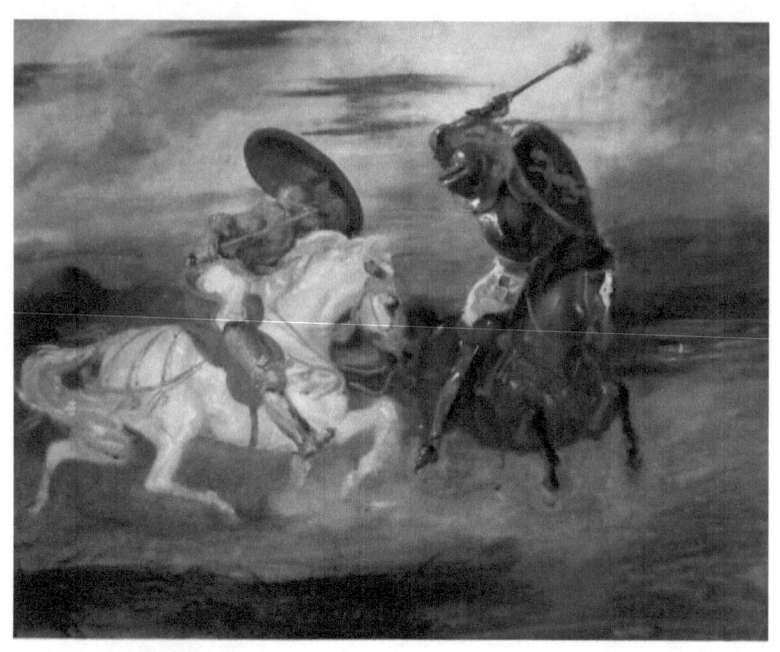

Confrontation of knights in the countryside, 1834
Oil on canvas

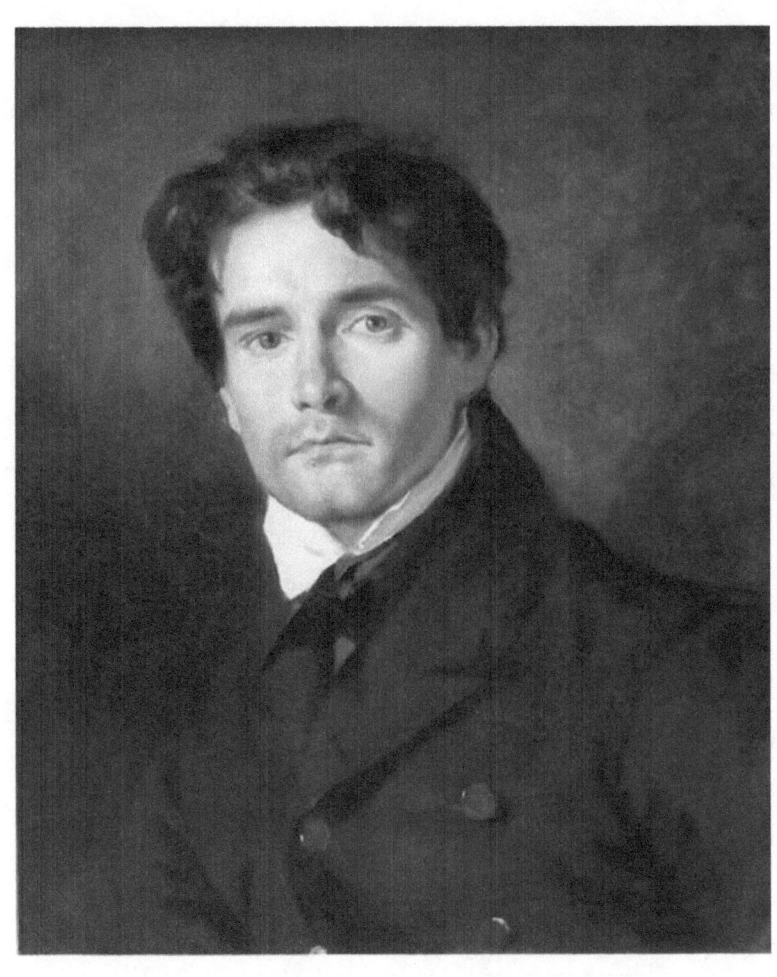

Léon Riesener, 1835
Oil on canvas

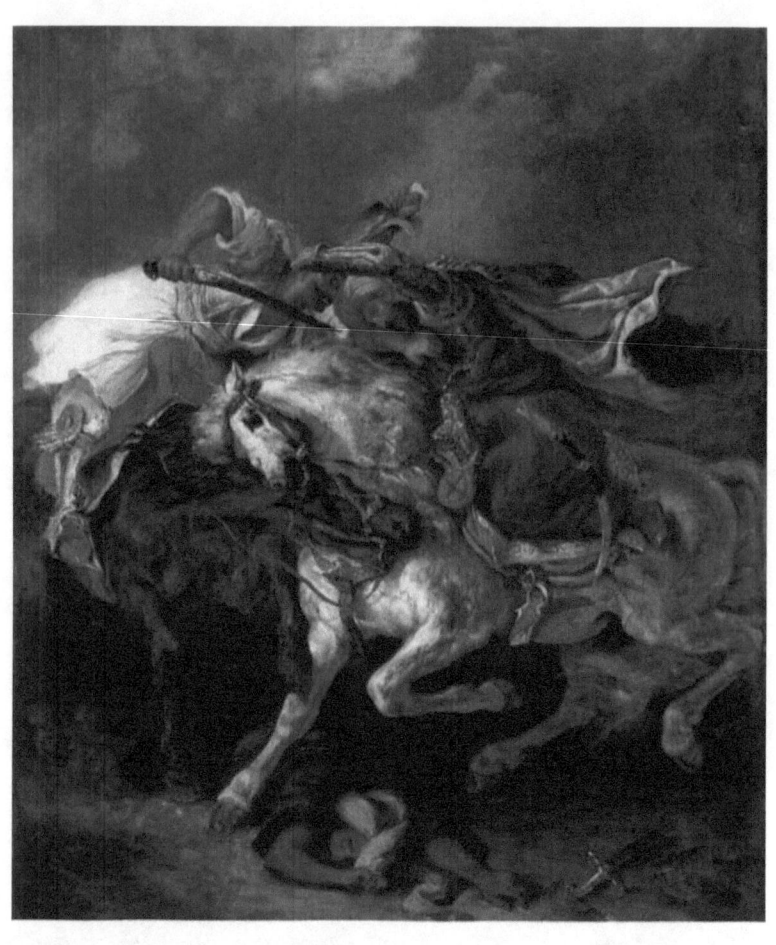

The Battle of Giaour and Hassan, 1835
Oil on canvas

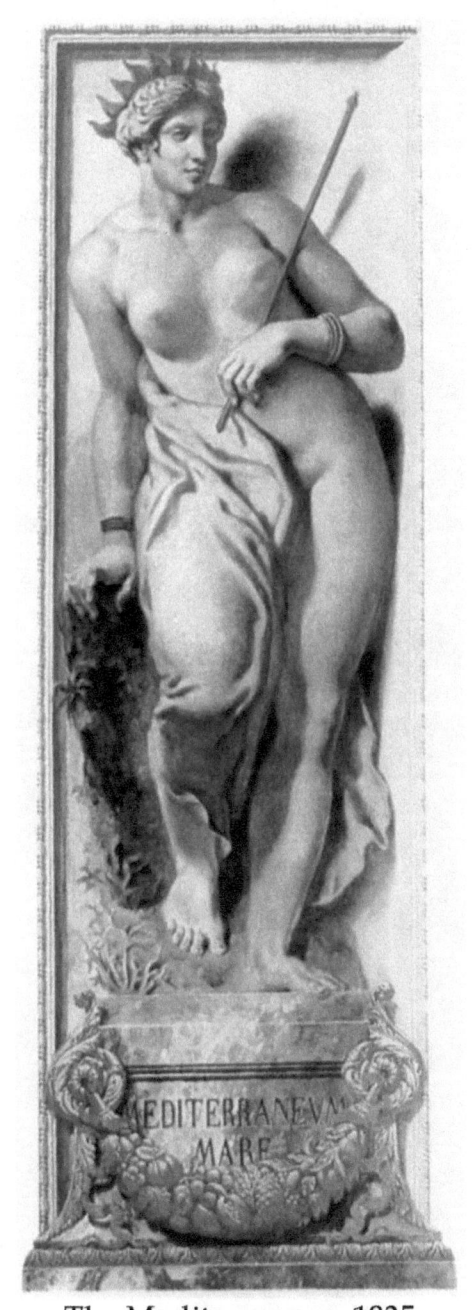

The Mediterranean, 1835

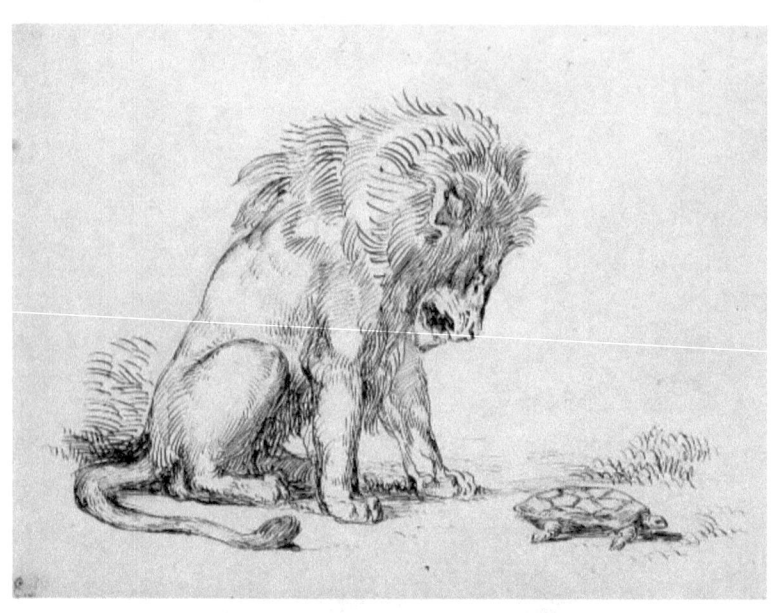

Lion and Tortoise, 1835
Pen, graphite, ink

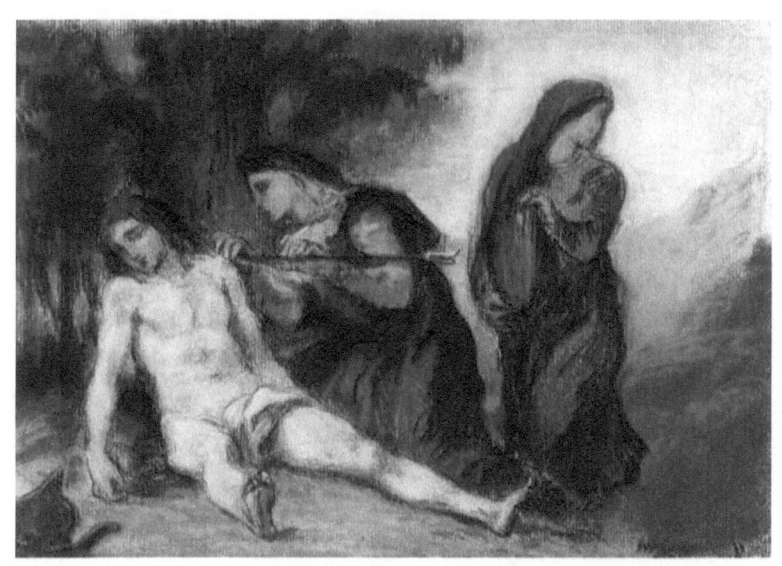

St. Sebastian, 1836
Oil on canvas

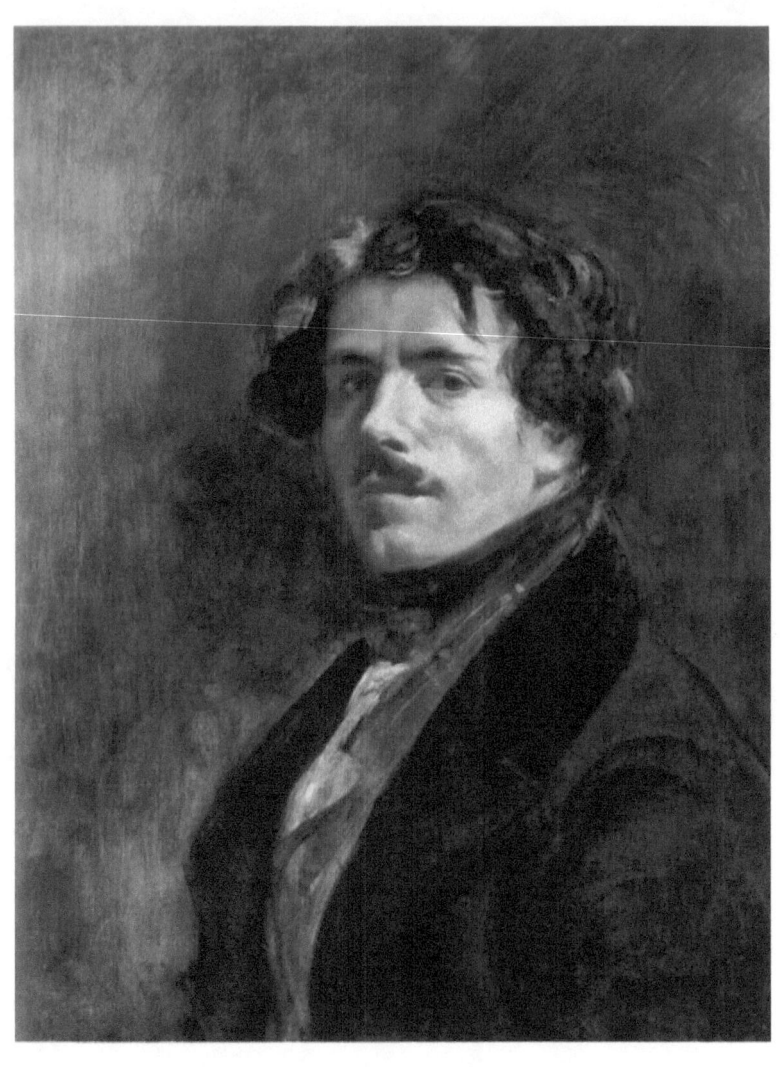

Self Portrait, c.1837
Oil on canvas

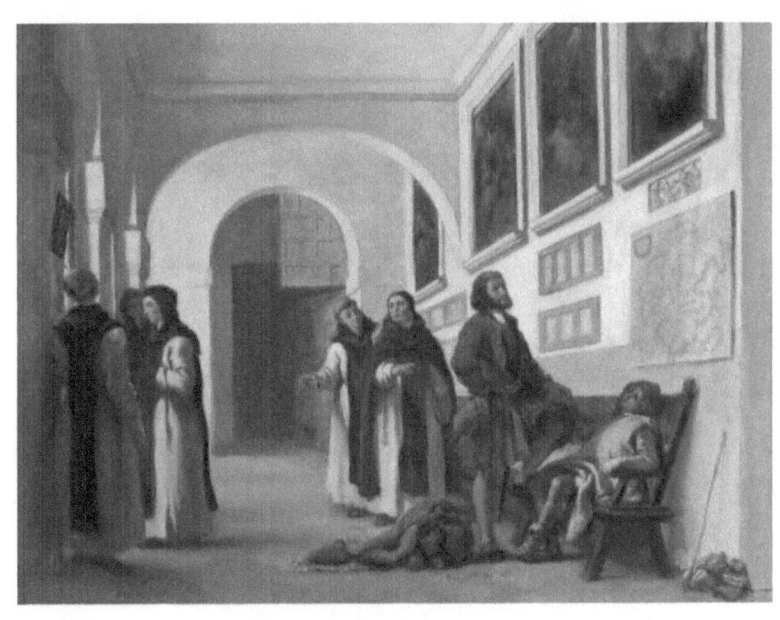

Christopher Columbus and His Son at La Rábida, 1838
Oil on canvas

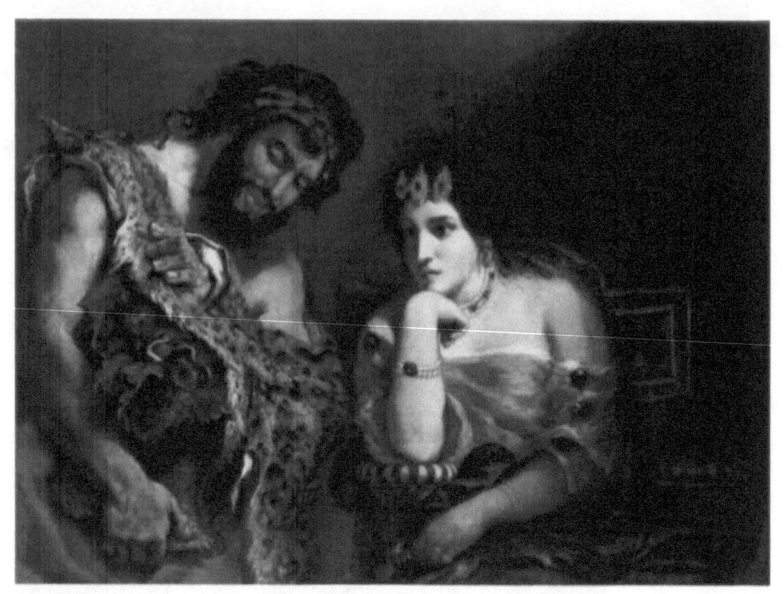

Cleopatra and the Peasant, 1838
Oil on canvas

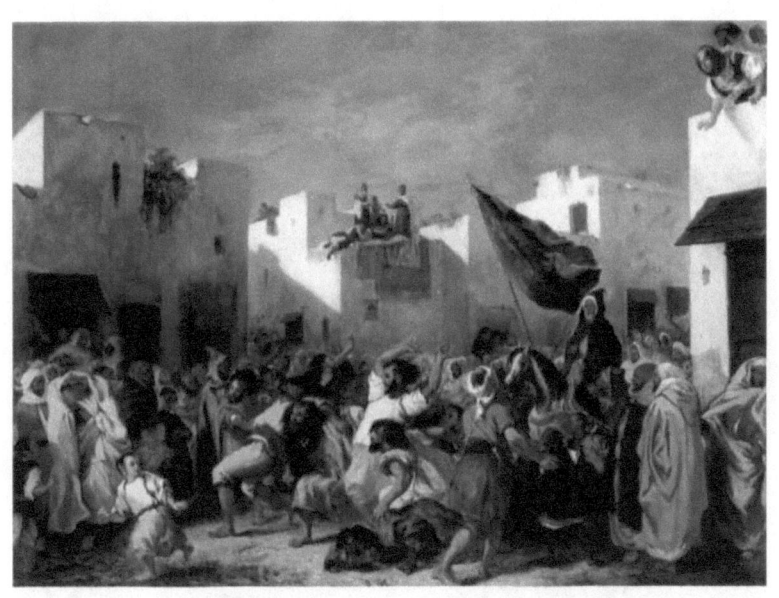

Fanatics of Tangier, 1837-1838
Oil on canvas

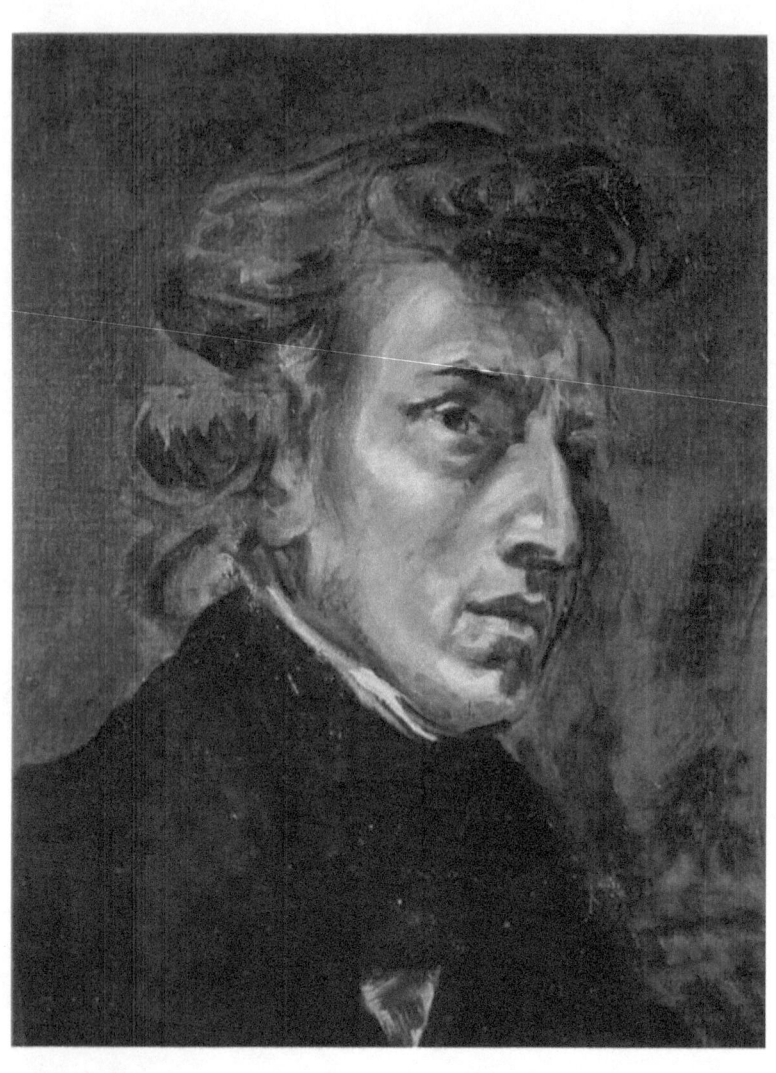

Frederic Chopin , 1838
Oil on canvas

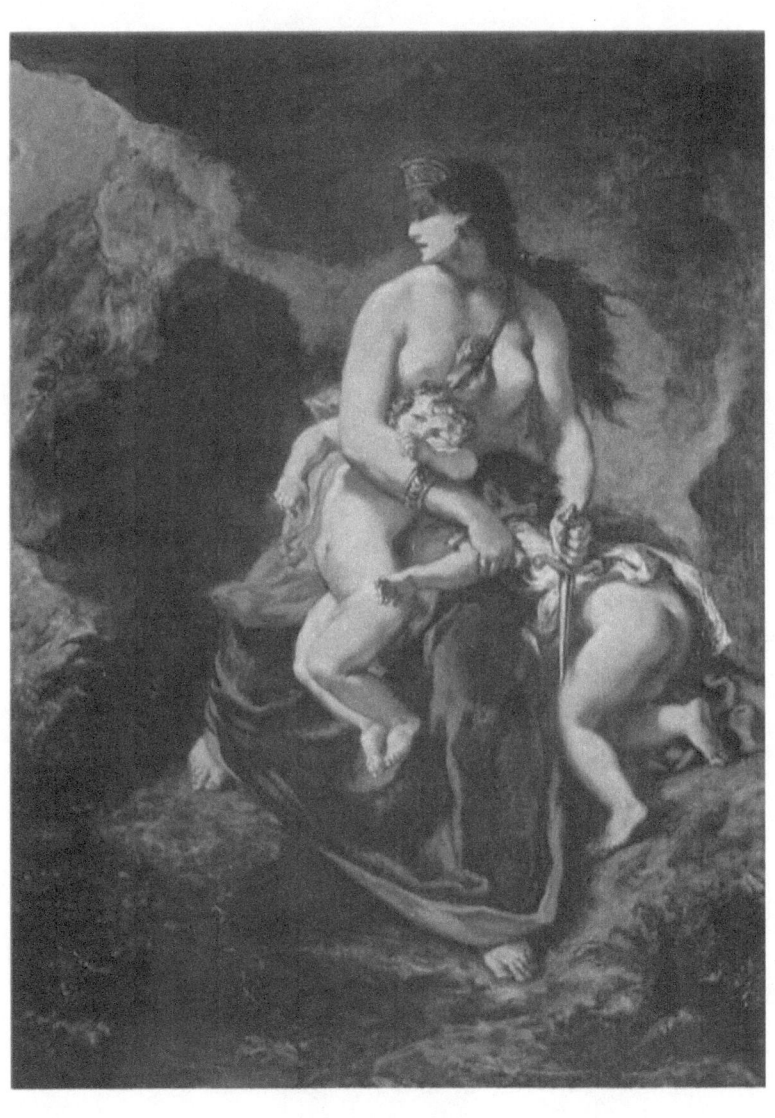

Medea, 1838
Oil on canvas

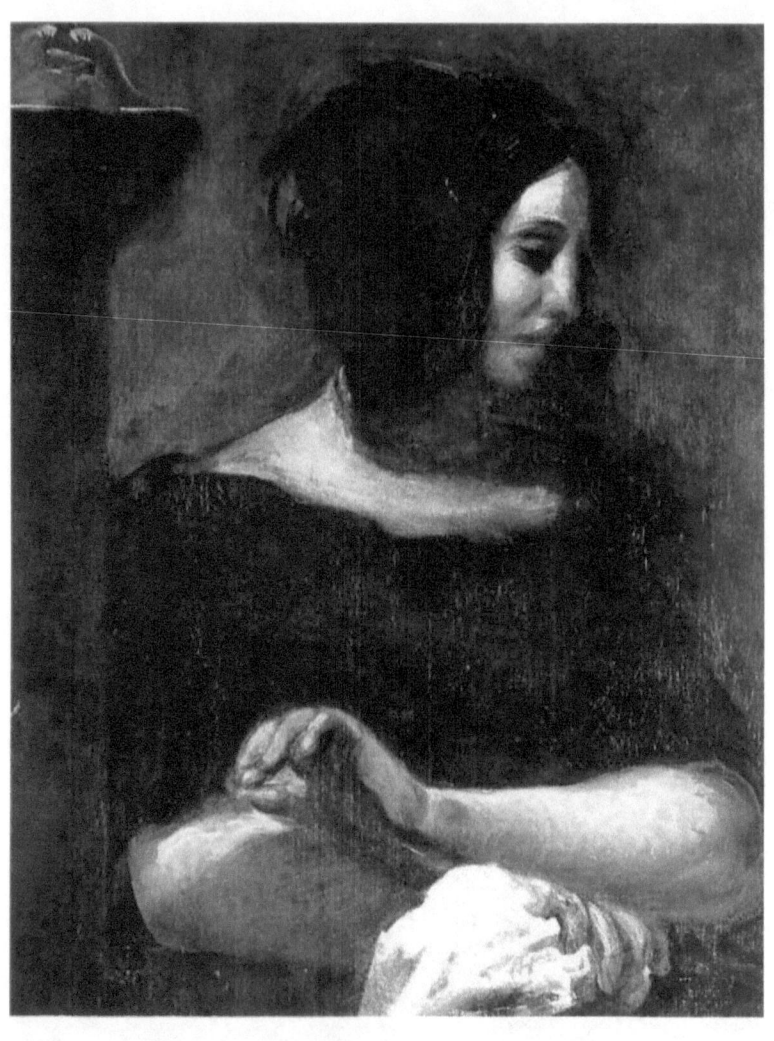

Portrait of George Sand, 1838
Oil on canvas

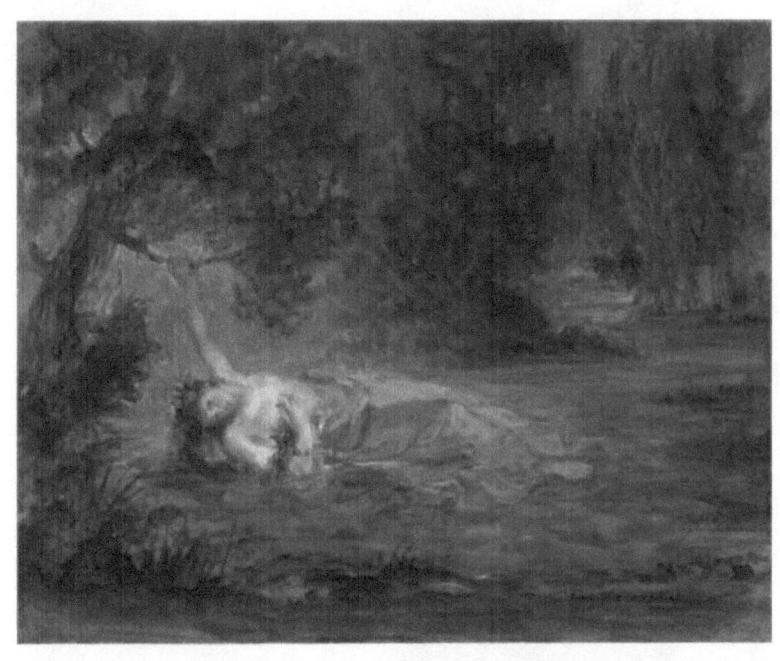

The Death of Ophelia, 1838
Oil on canvas

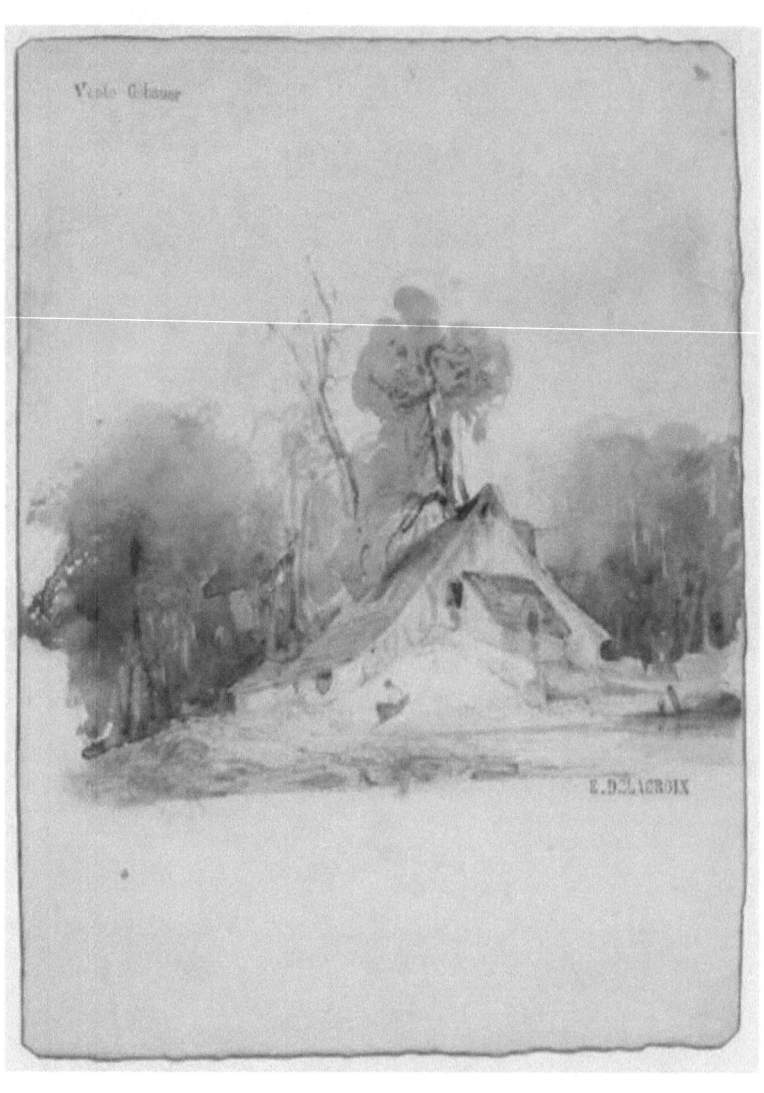

The Cottage in the grove, 1838
Chalk, ink

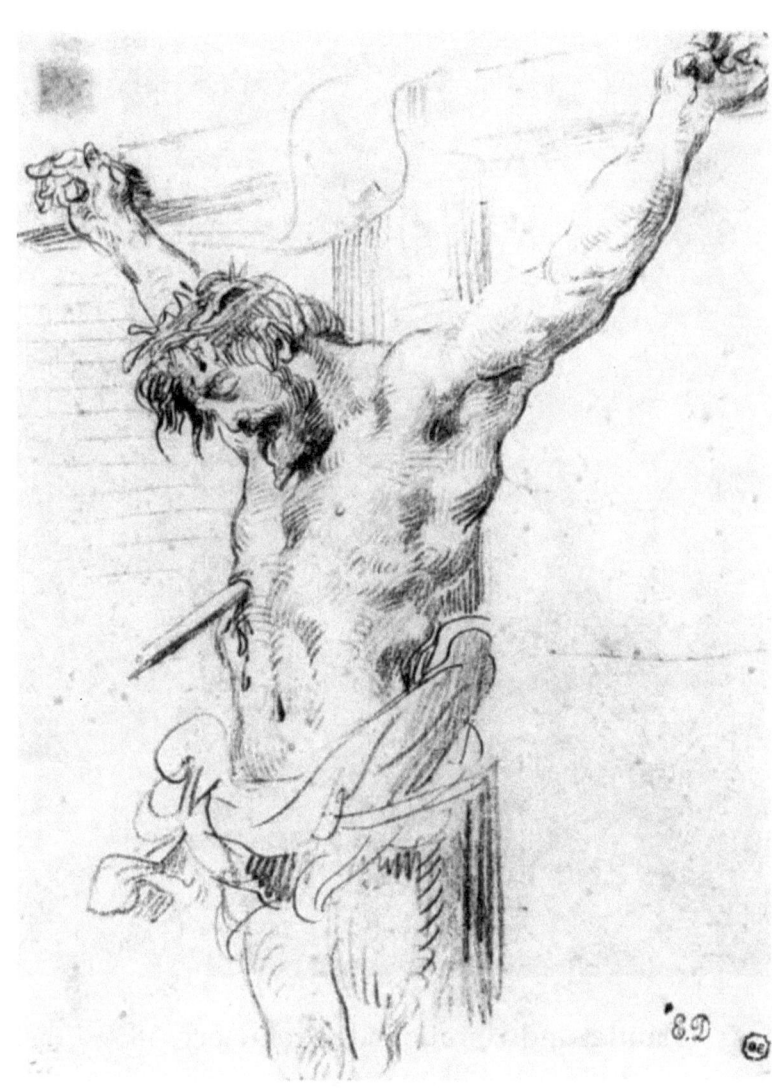

Christ on the Cross, 1839

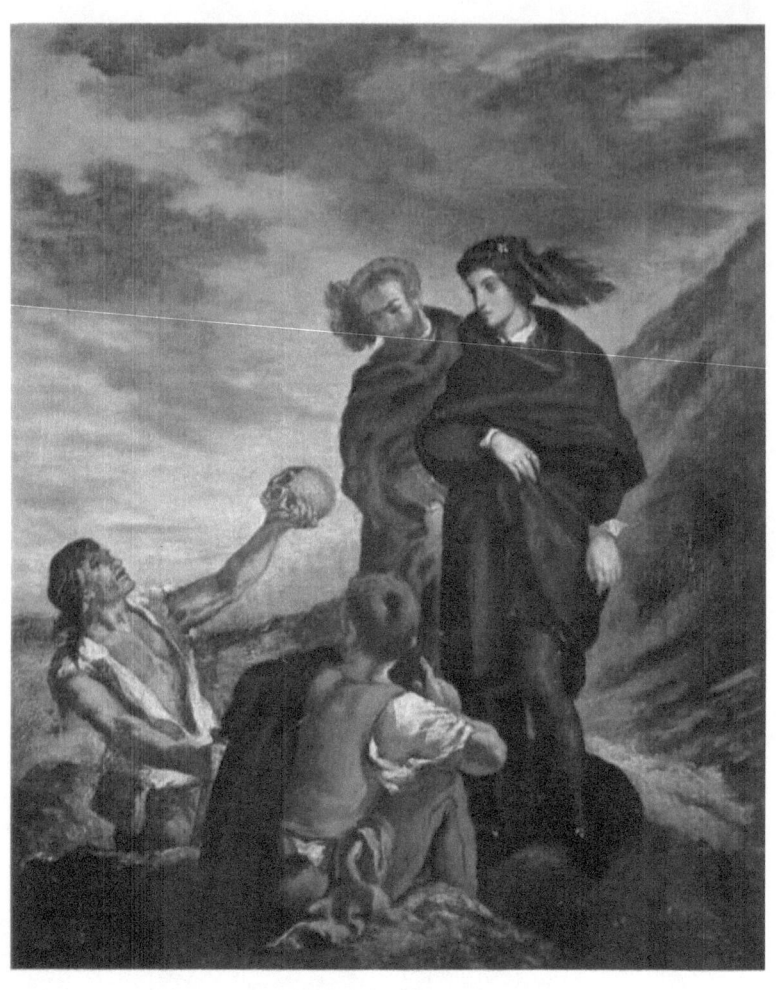

Hamlet and Horatio in the cemetery, 1839
Oil on canvas

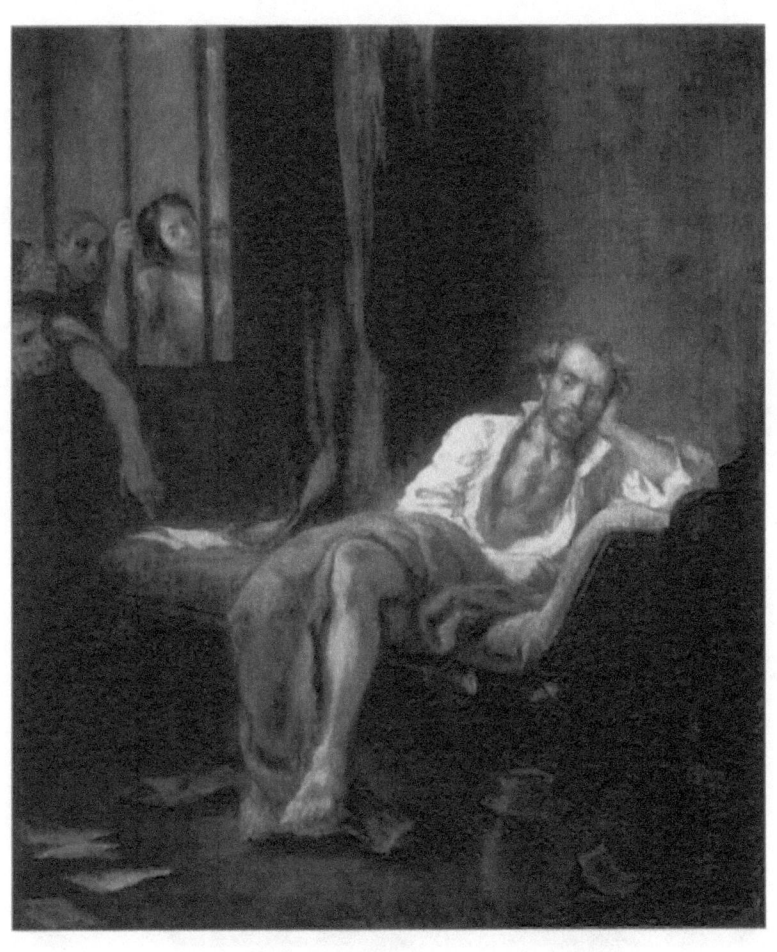

Tasso in the Madhouse, 1839
Oil on canvas

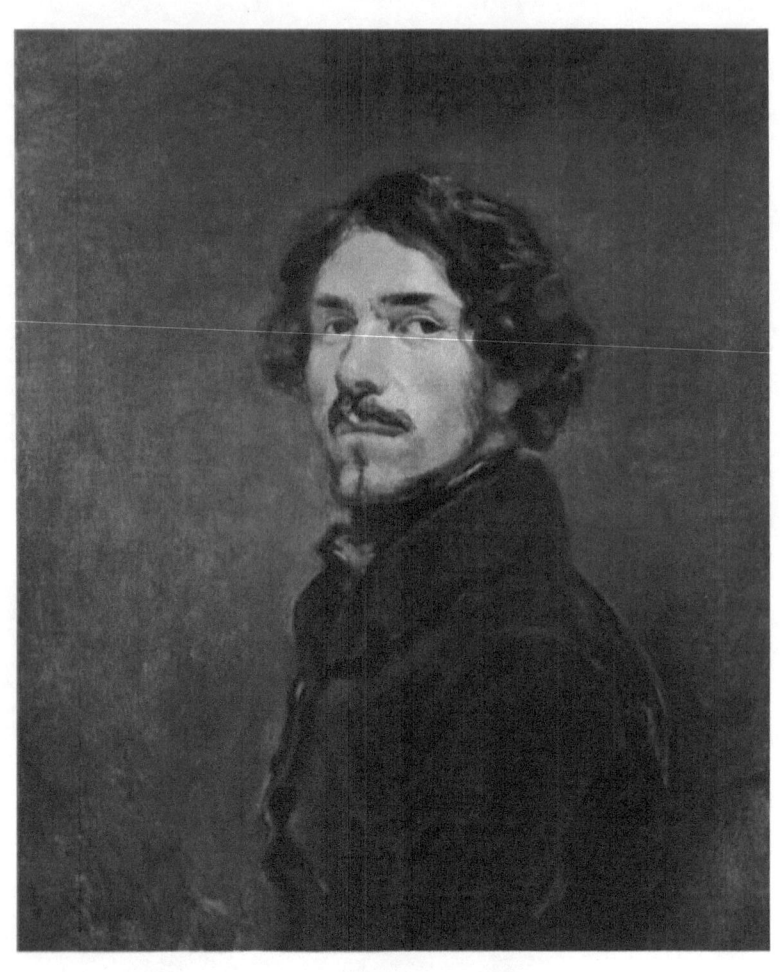

Self Portrait, c.1840
Oil on canvas

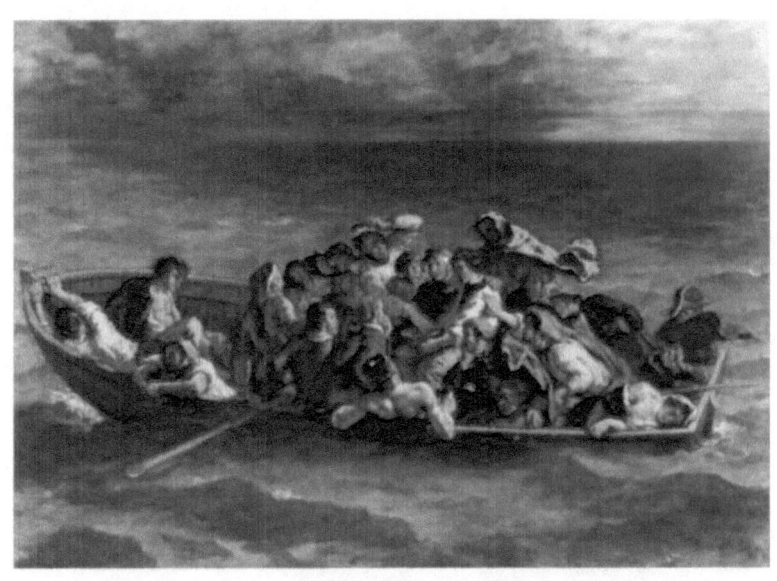

The Shipwreck of Don Juan, 1840
Oil on canvas

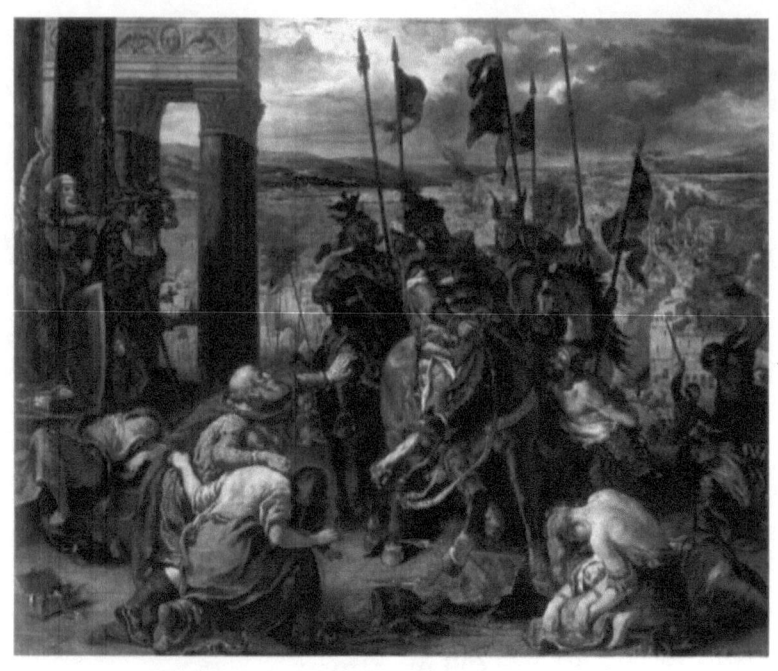

The Crusaders' entry into Constantinople, 12th April
1204, 1840 (oil on canvas), 1840
Oil on canvas

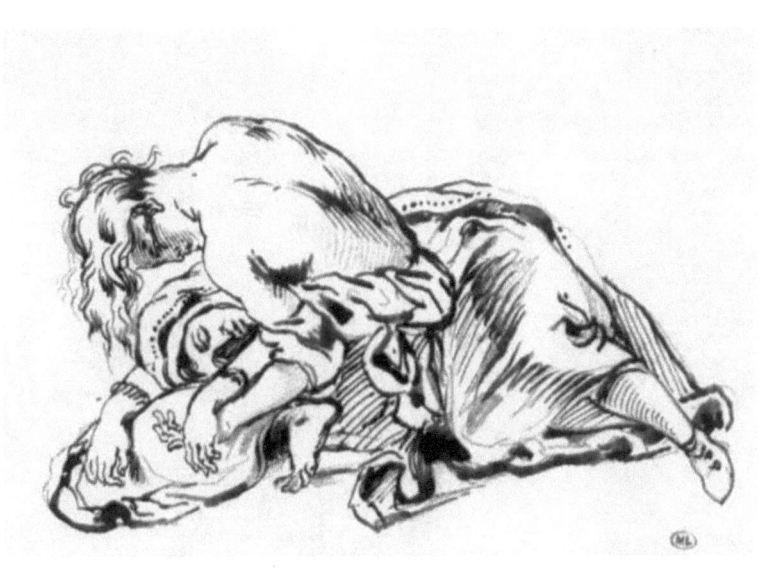

Young Woman Leaning over a Woman Stretched out
on the Ground, c. 1840
Pen and wash

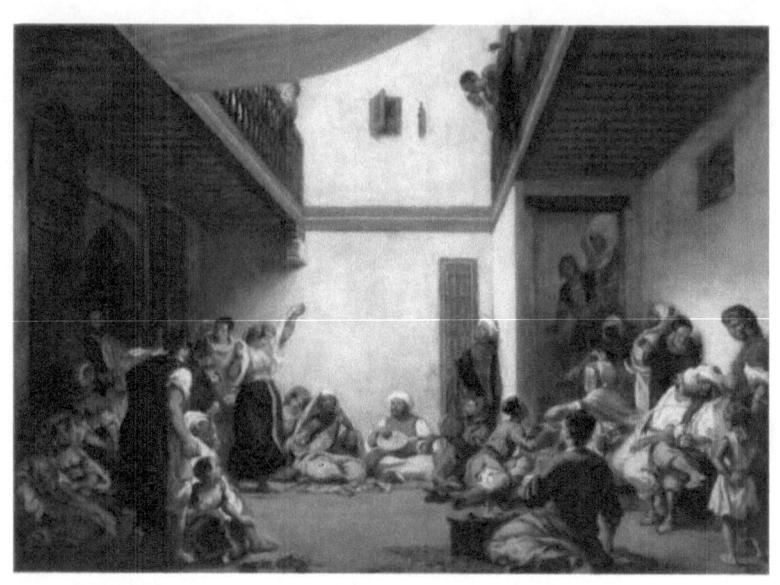

A Jewish wedding in Morocco, 1841
Oil on canvas

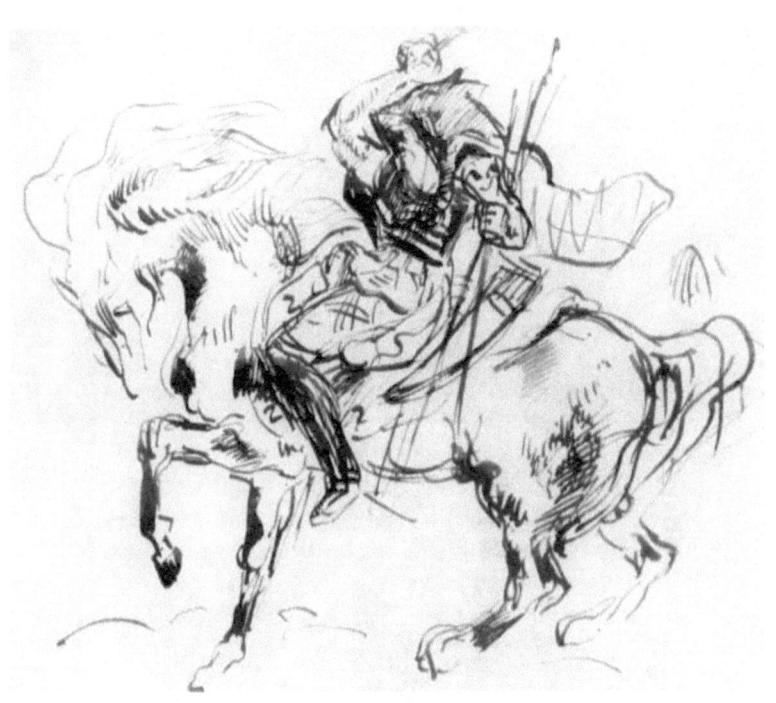

Sketch for Attila, 1843-47
Pen and brown ink on paper,

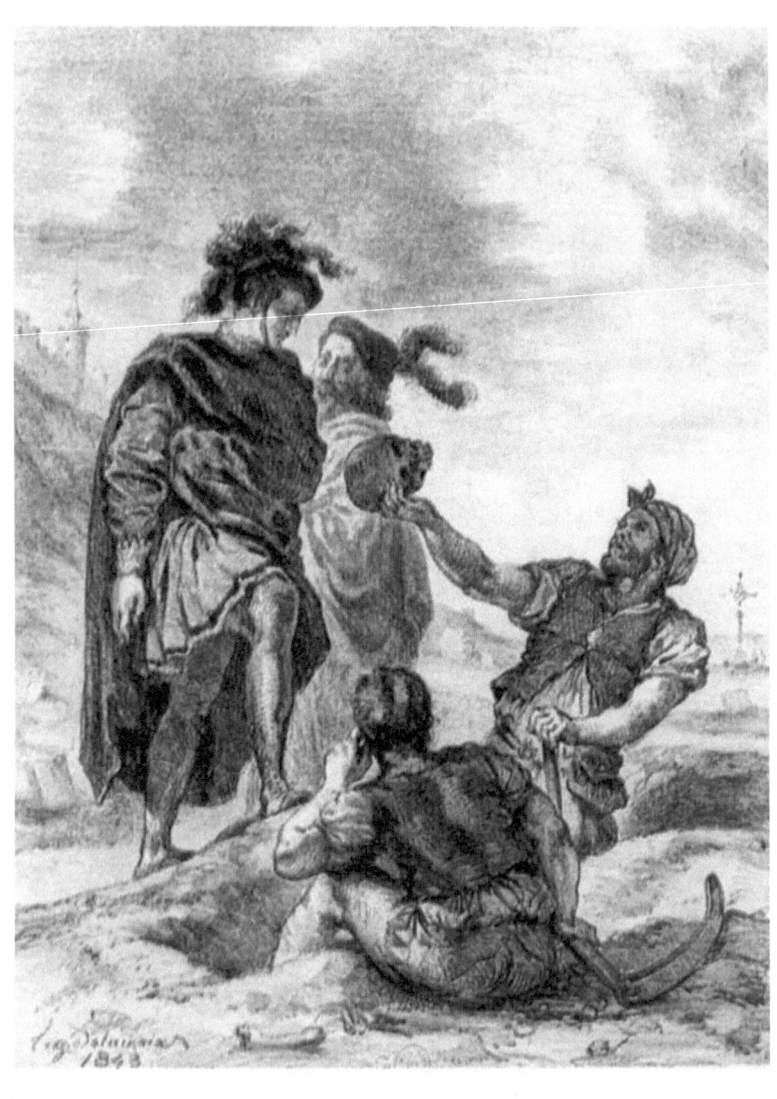

Hamlet and Horatio in the Graveyard, 1843
Lithograph, 283 x 214 mm

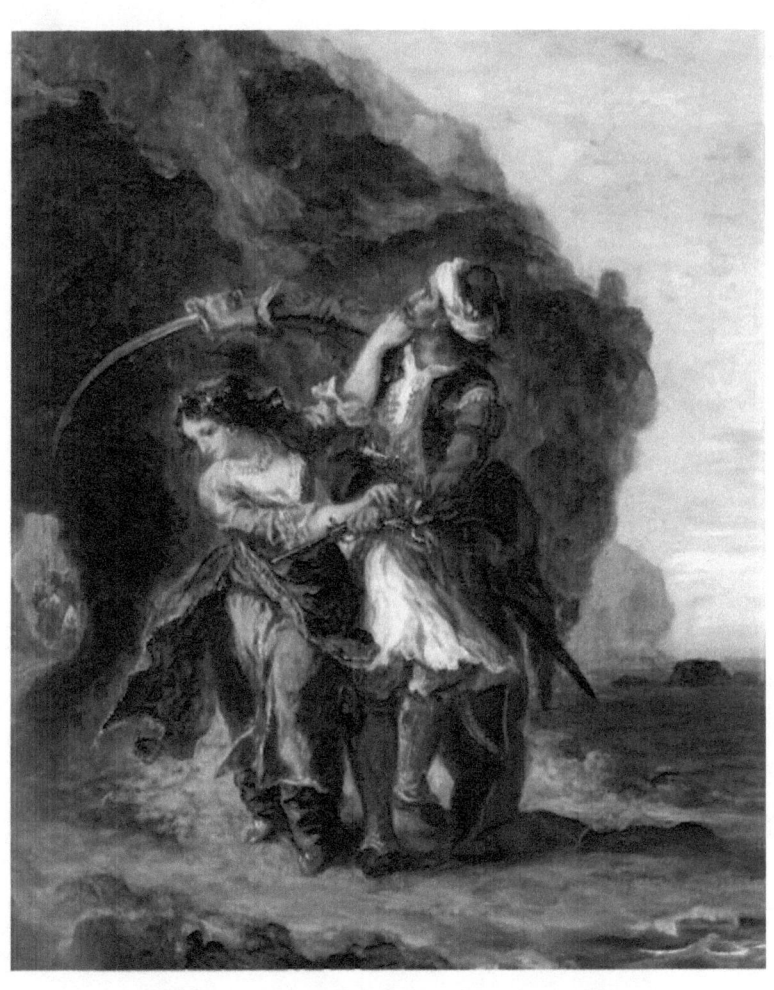

The Bride of Abydos, 1843
Oil on canvas

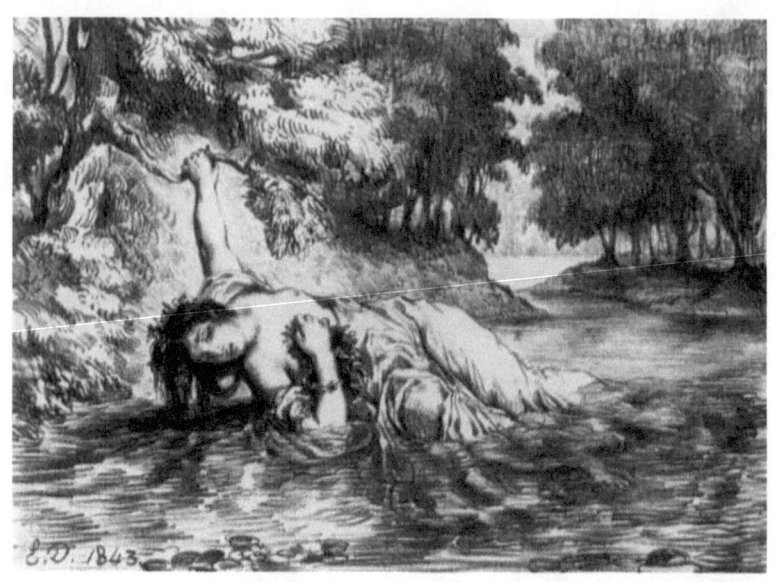

The Death of Ophelia, 1843

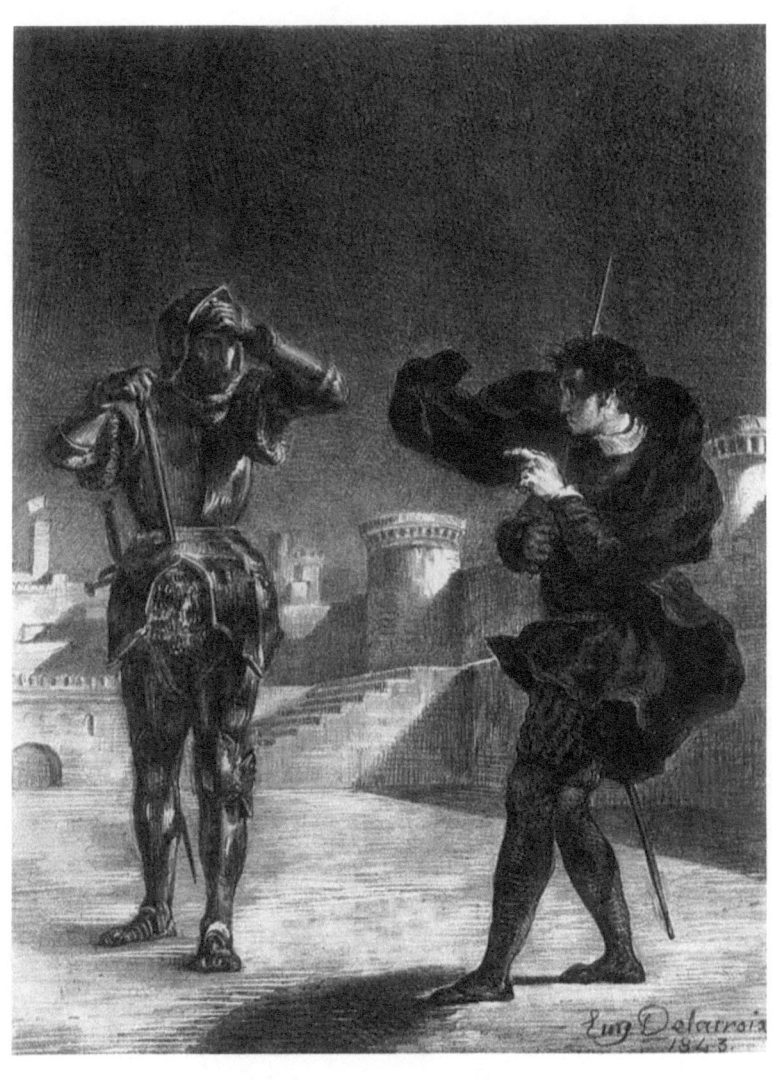

Hamlet Sees the Ghost of his Father, 1843

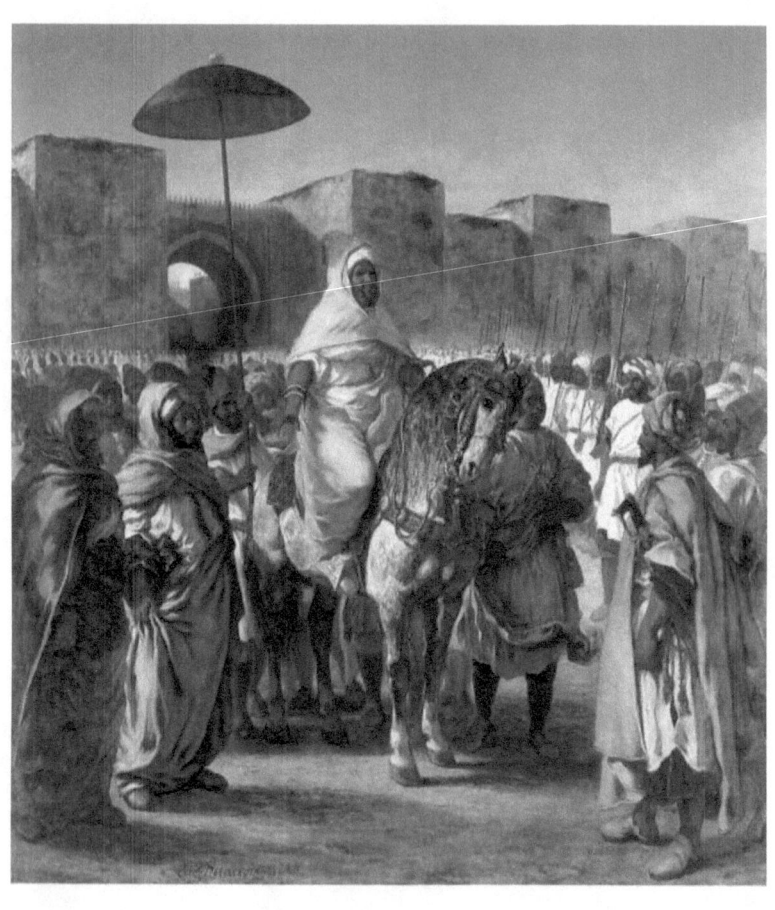

Muley Abd-ar-Rhaman, The Sultan of Morocco, leaving
his Palace of Meknes with his entourage, 1845
Oil on canvas

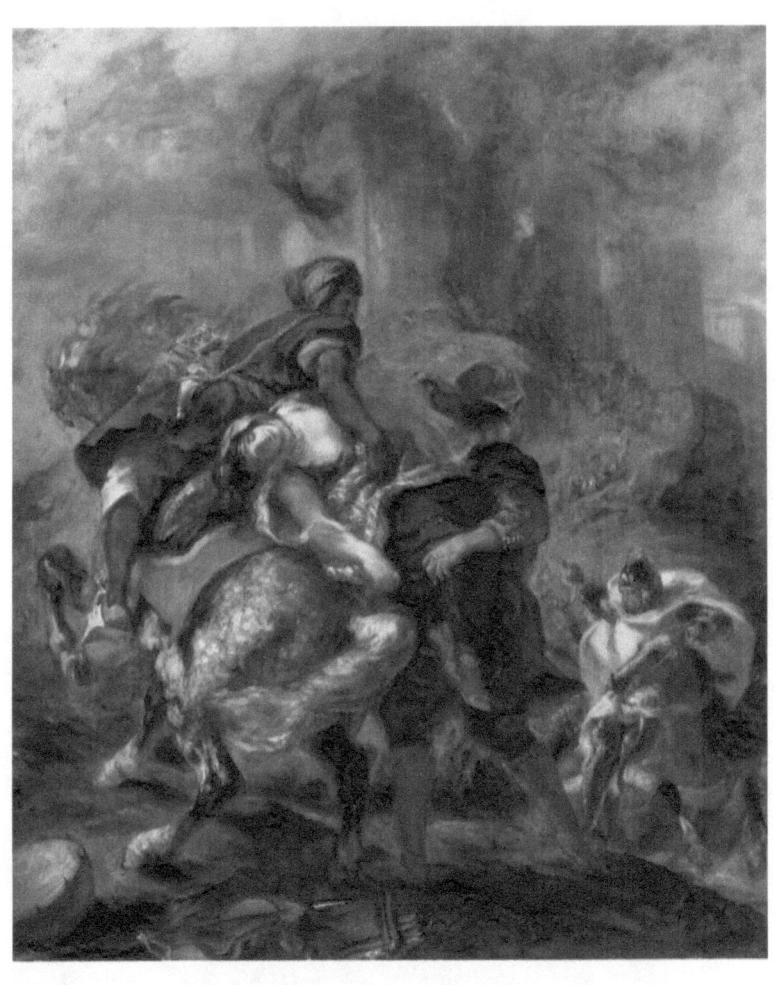

The Abduction of Rebecca, 1846
Oil on canvas

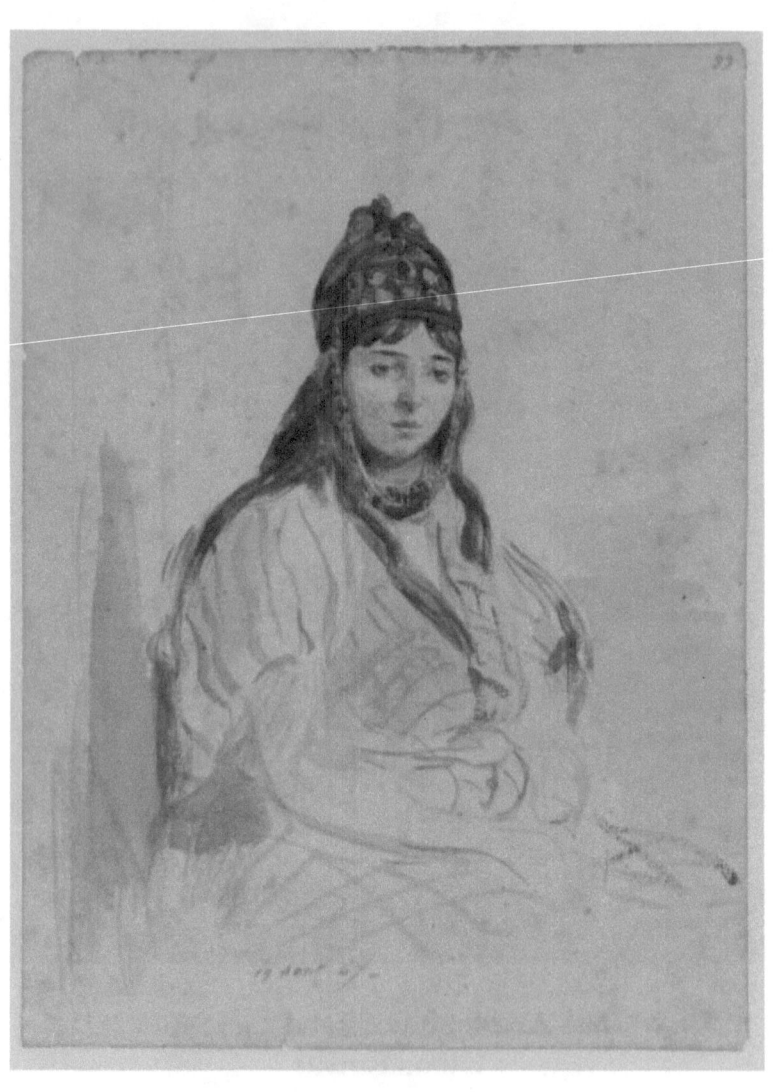

A North African Jewess, 1847
Watercolor

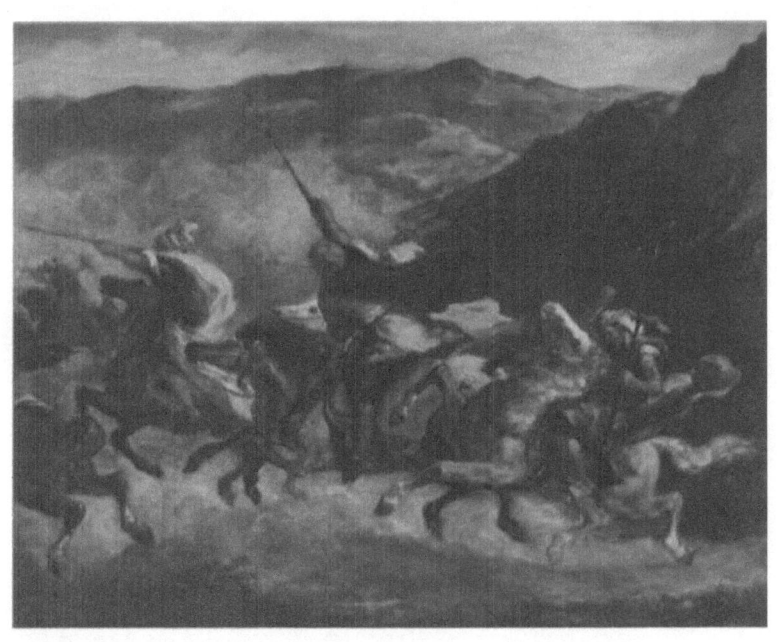

Moroccan Fantasia, 1847
Oil on canvas

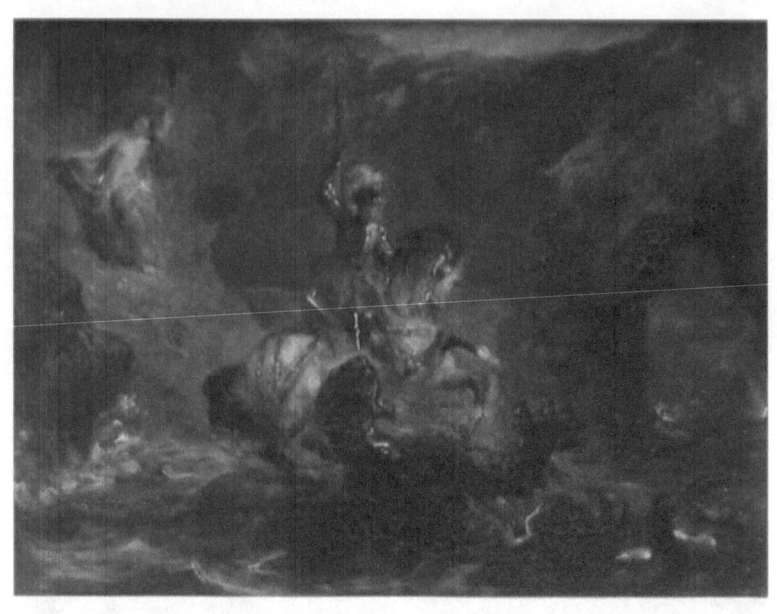

Saint George Fighting the Dragon, Perseus Delivering
Andromeda, 1847
Oil on canvas

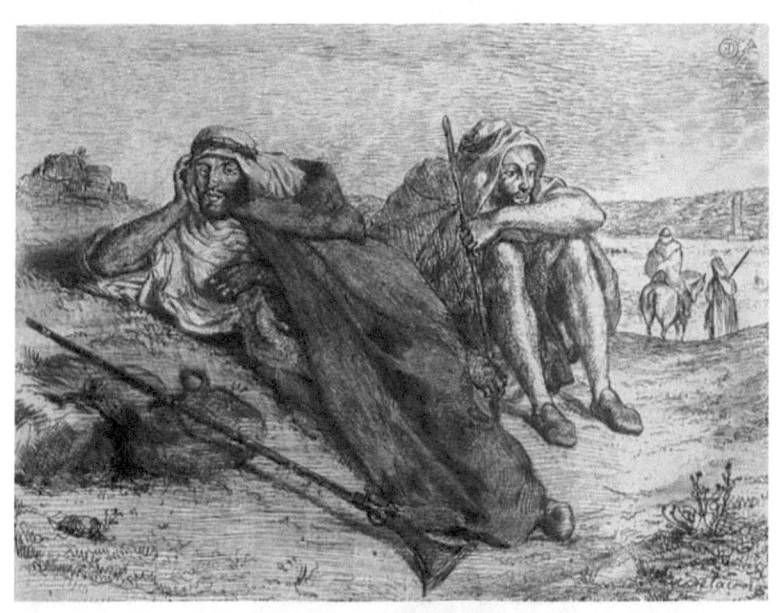

Arabs of Oran, 1833-1847
Lithography

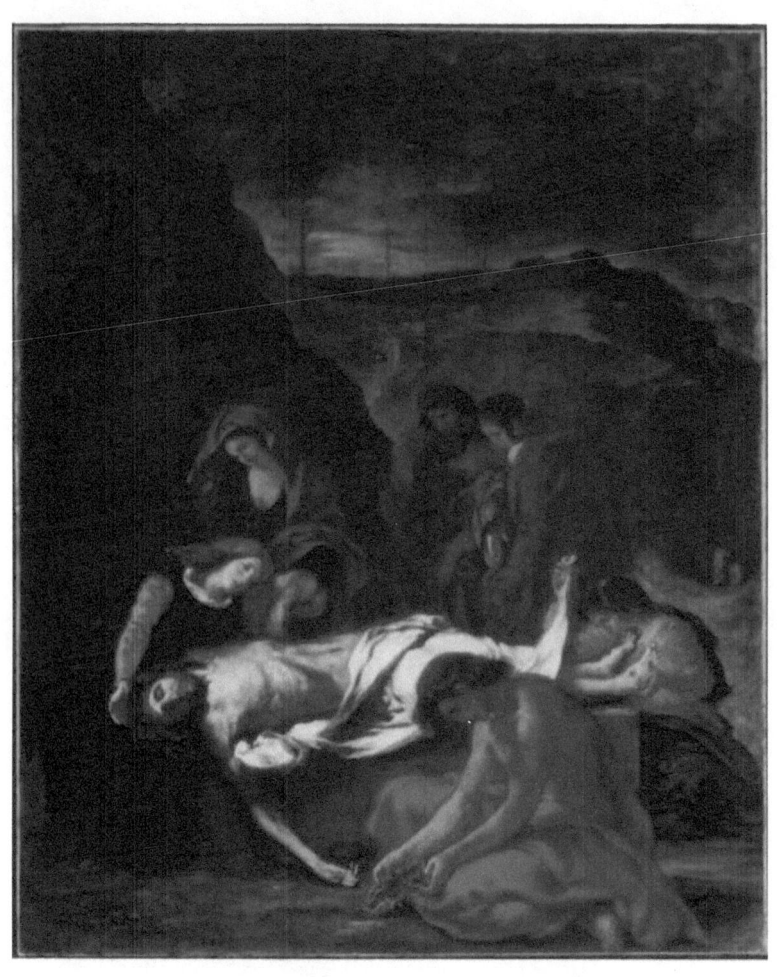

The Entombment of Christ, 1848
Oil on canvas

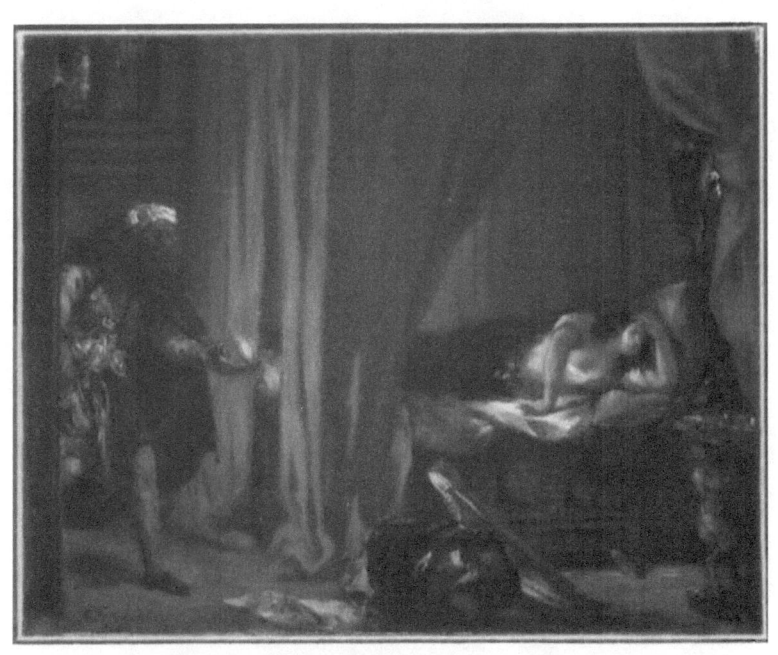

Othello and Desdemona, 1847-1849
Oil on canvas

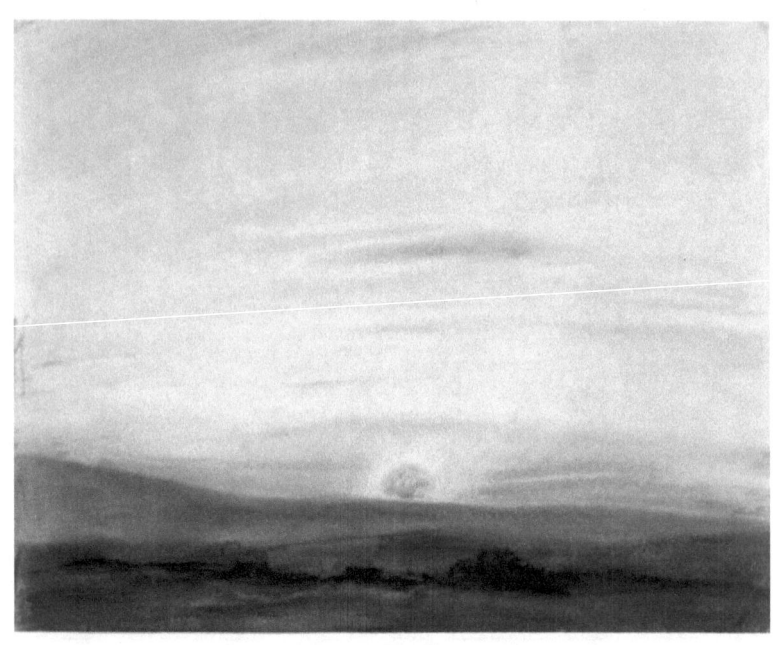

Study of Sky, Setting Sun, 1849
Pastel

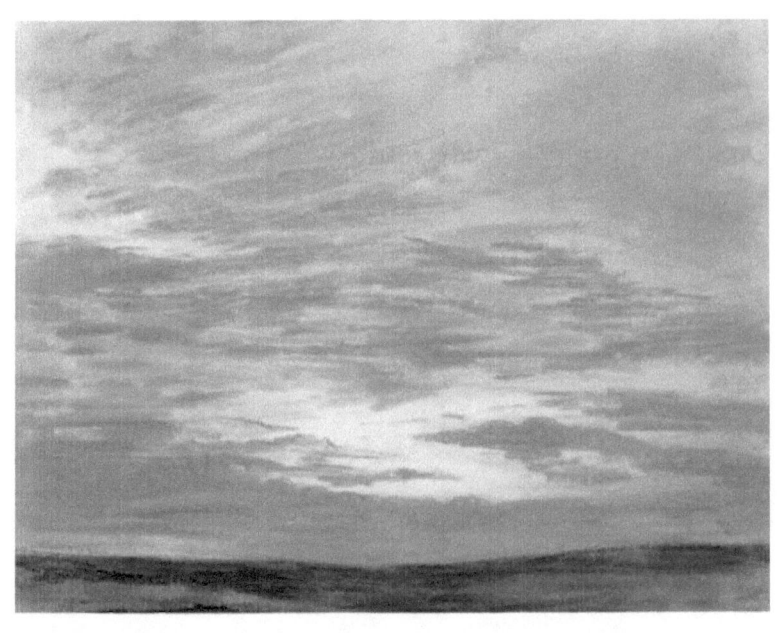

Study of the Sky at Sunset, 1849
Pastel

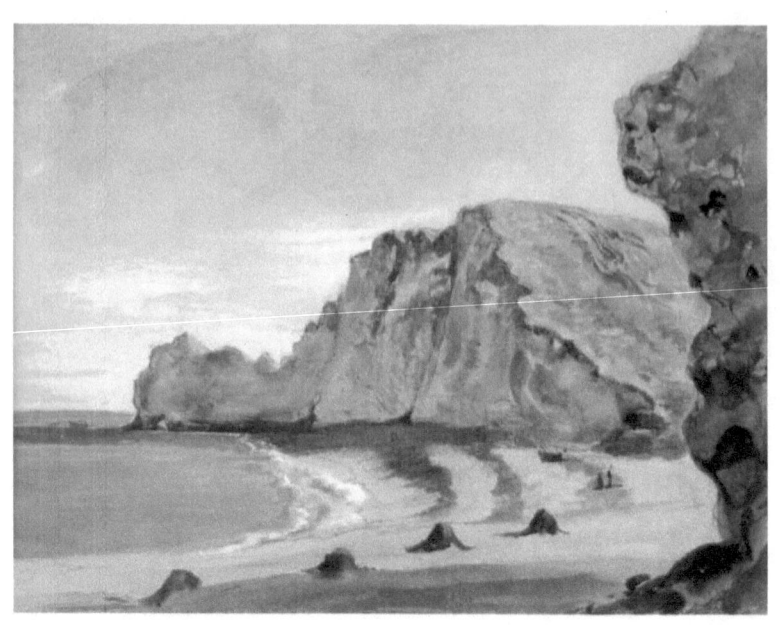

The Porte d'Amont, Etretat, 1849
Pastel

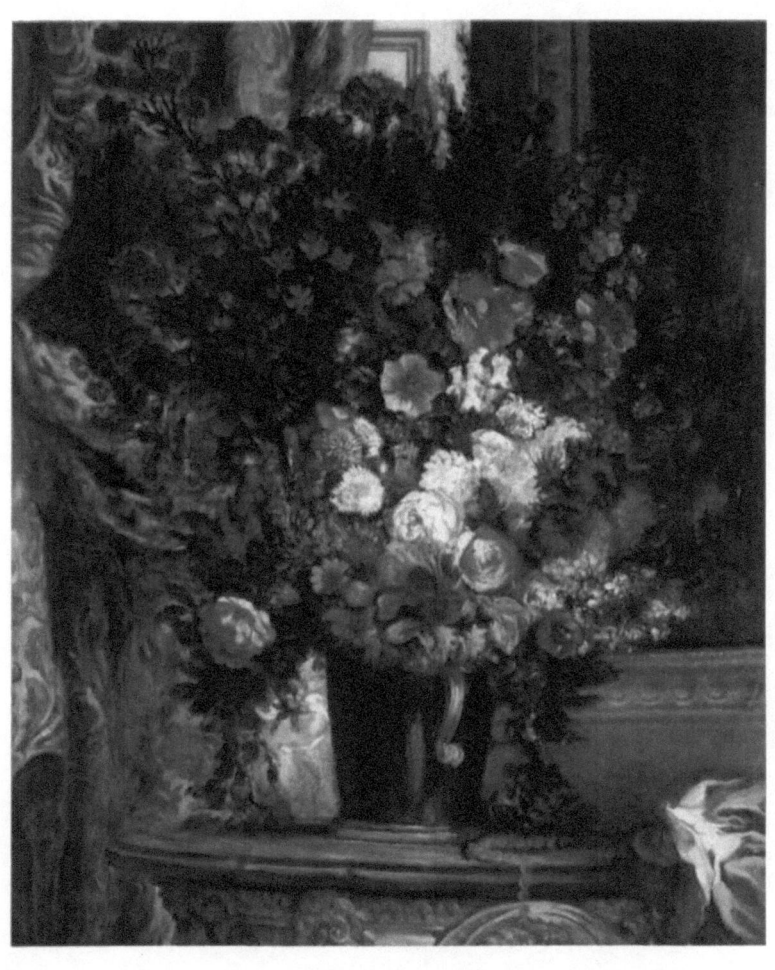

Vase of Flowers on a Console, 1848-1849
Oil on canvas

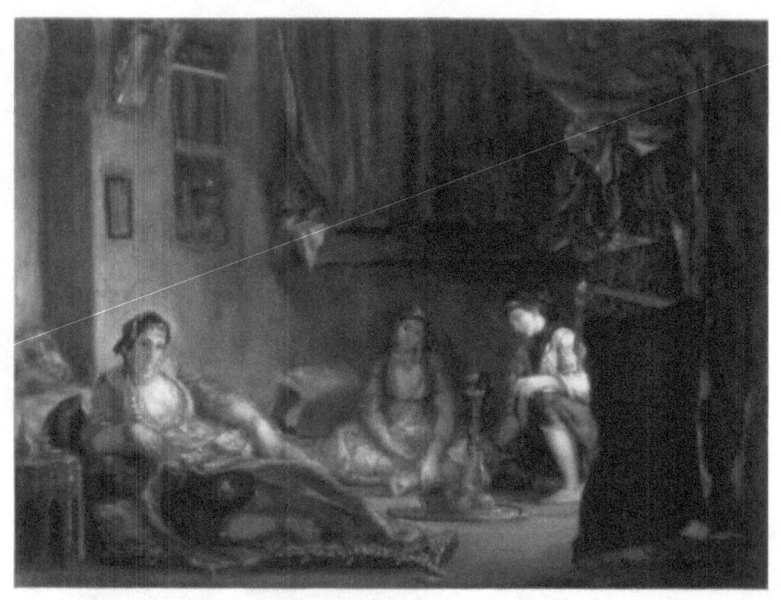

Women of Algiers in Their Apartment, 1849
Oil on canvas

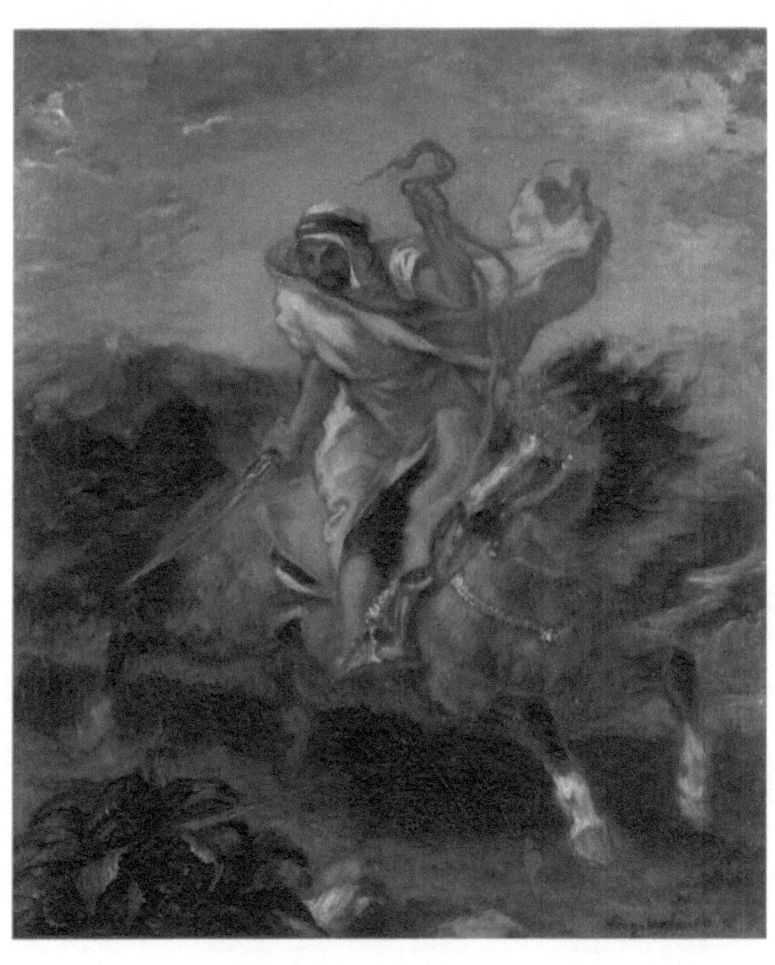

An Arab Horseman at the Gallop, 1849
Oil on canvas

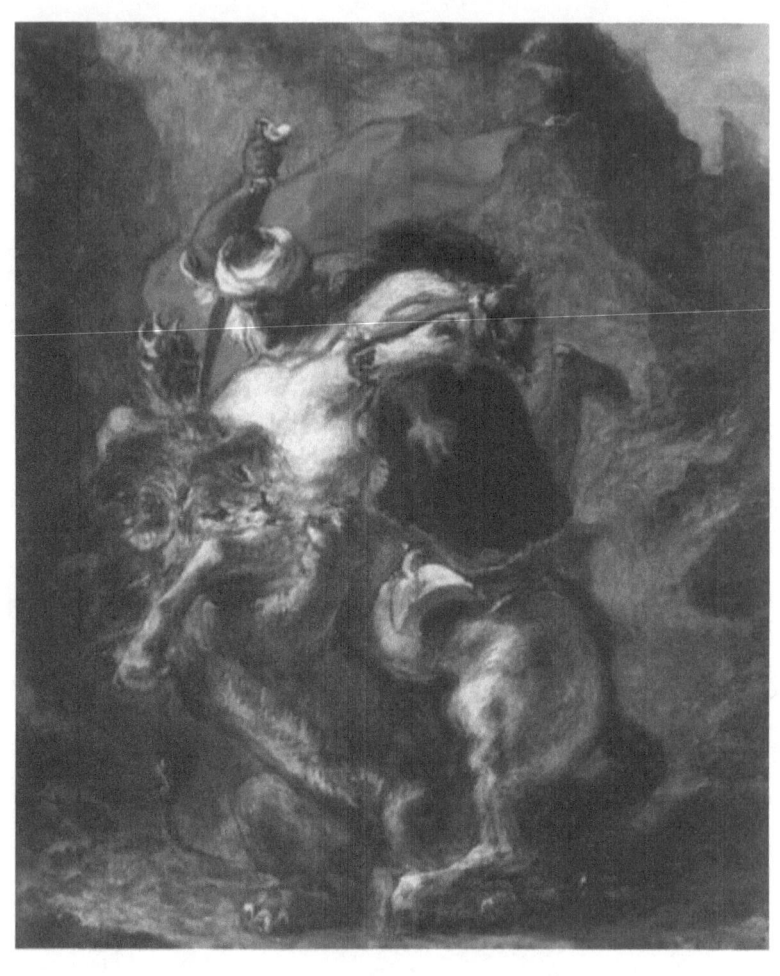

Arab Horseman Attacked by Lion, 1849-1850
Oil on panel

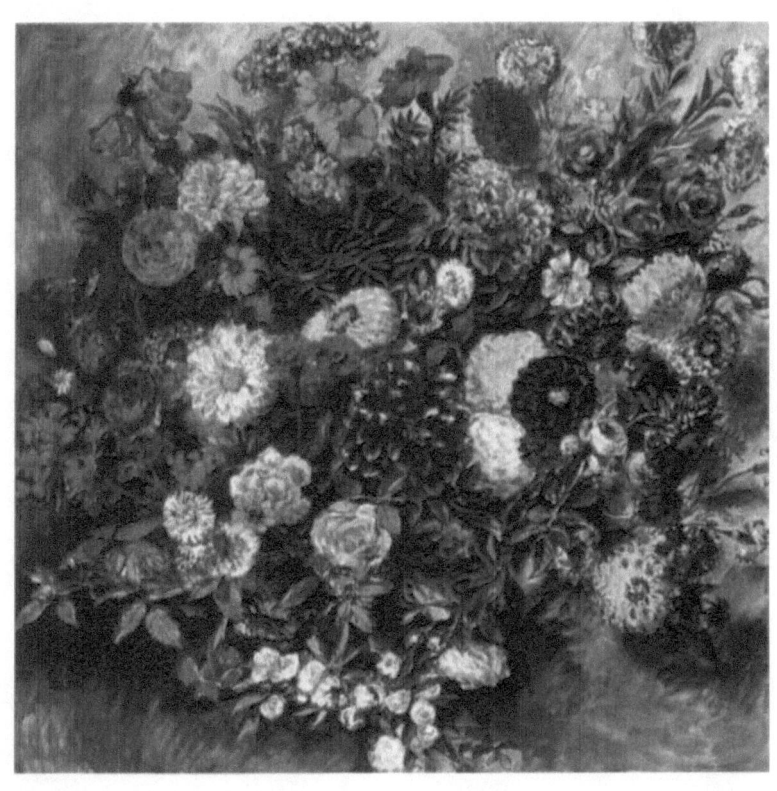

Bouquet of Flowers, 1849-1850
Gouache, watercolor

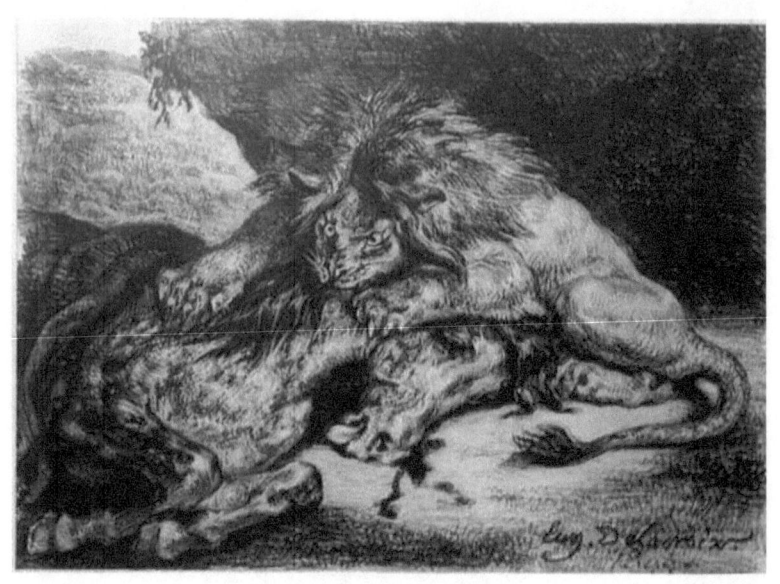

Lion devouring an Arab horse, 1850

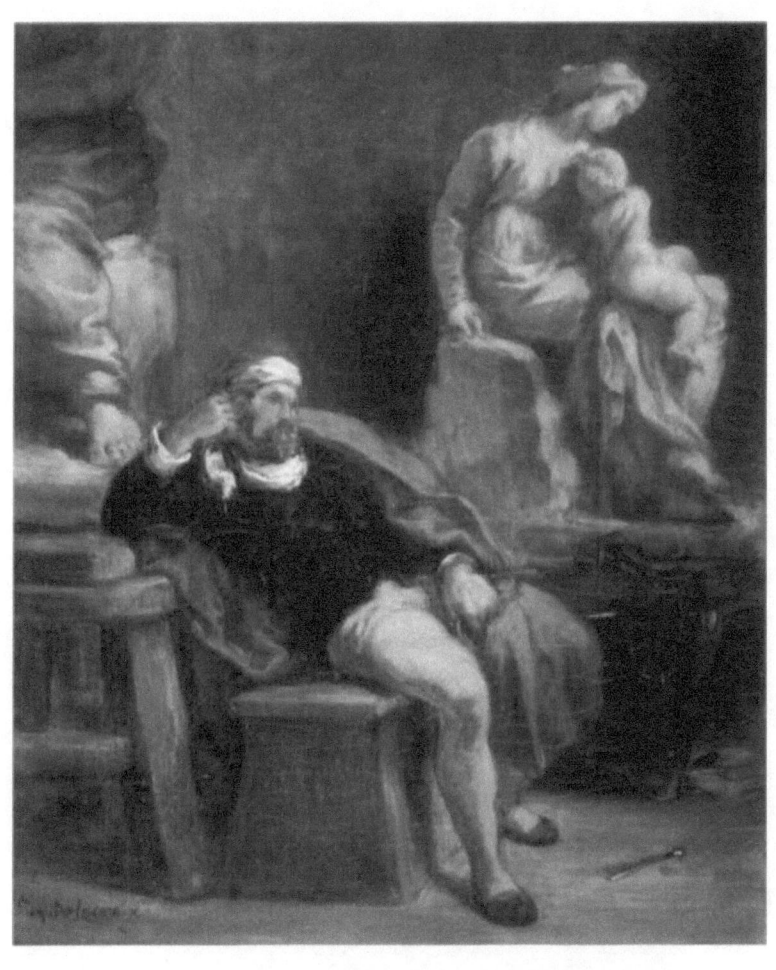

Michelangelo in his Studio , 1849-1850
Oil on canvas

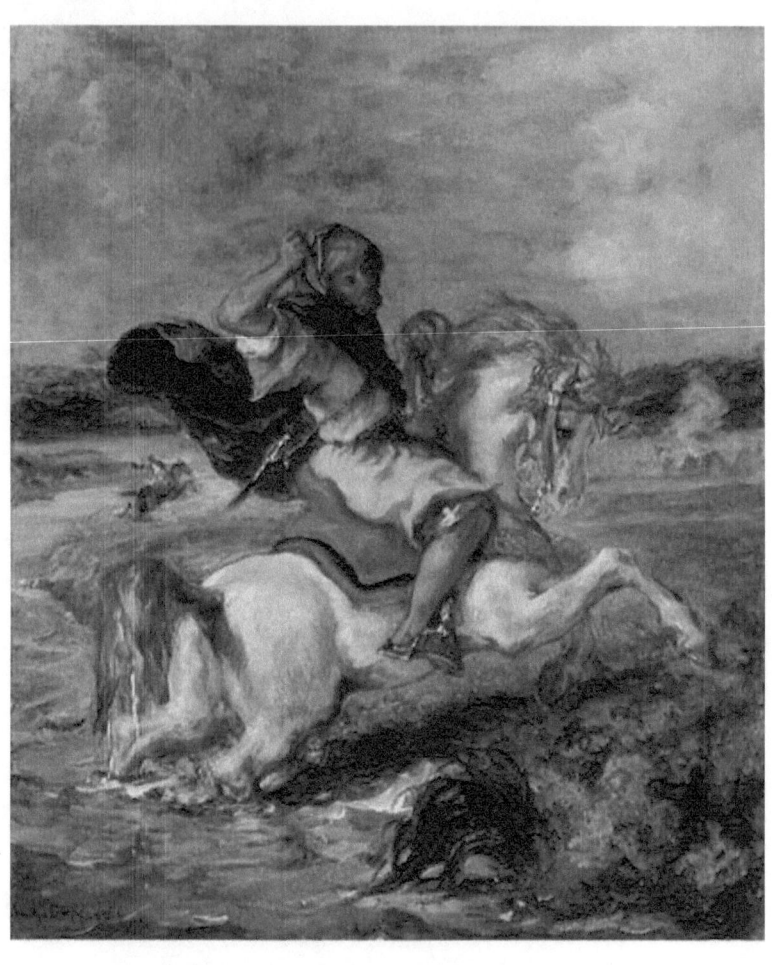

Moroccan Horseman Crossing a Ford, 1850
Oil on canvas

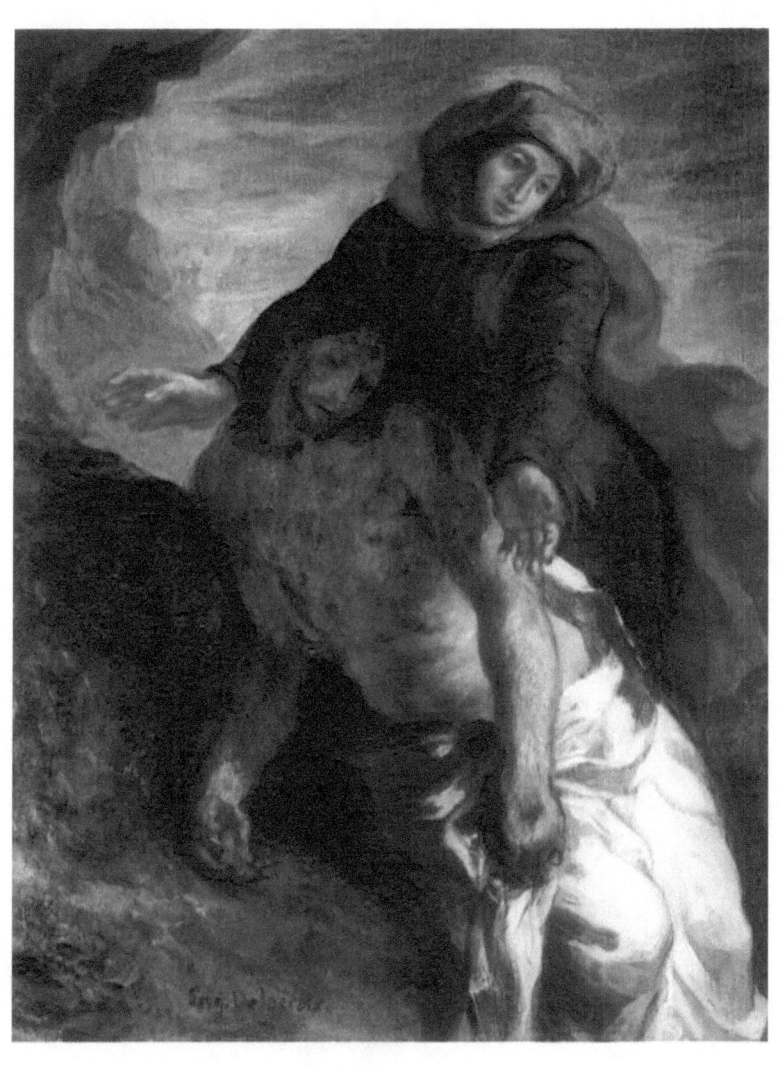

Pietà, 1850
Oil on canvas

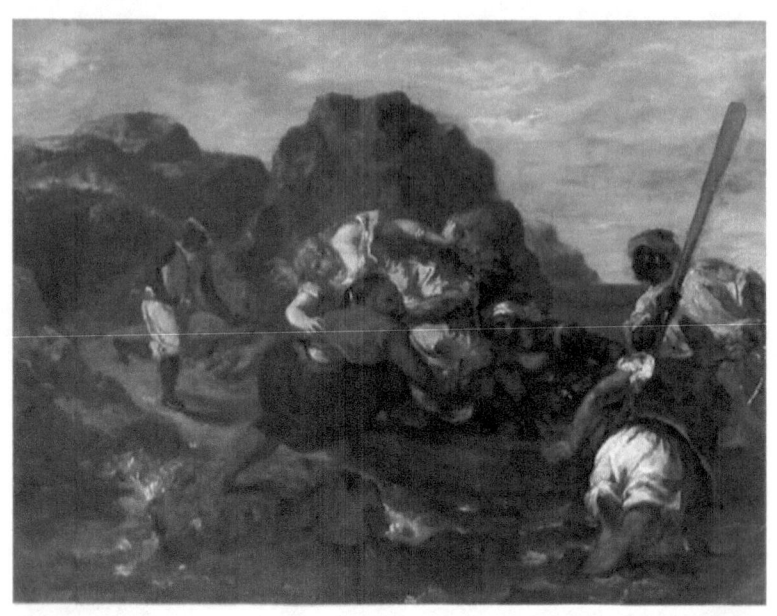

African Pirates Abducting a Young Woman, 1852
Oil on canvas

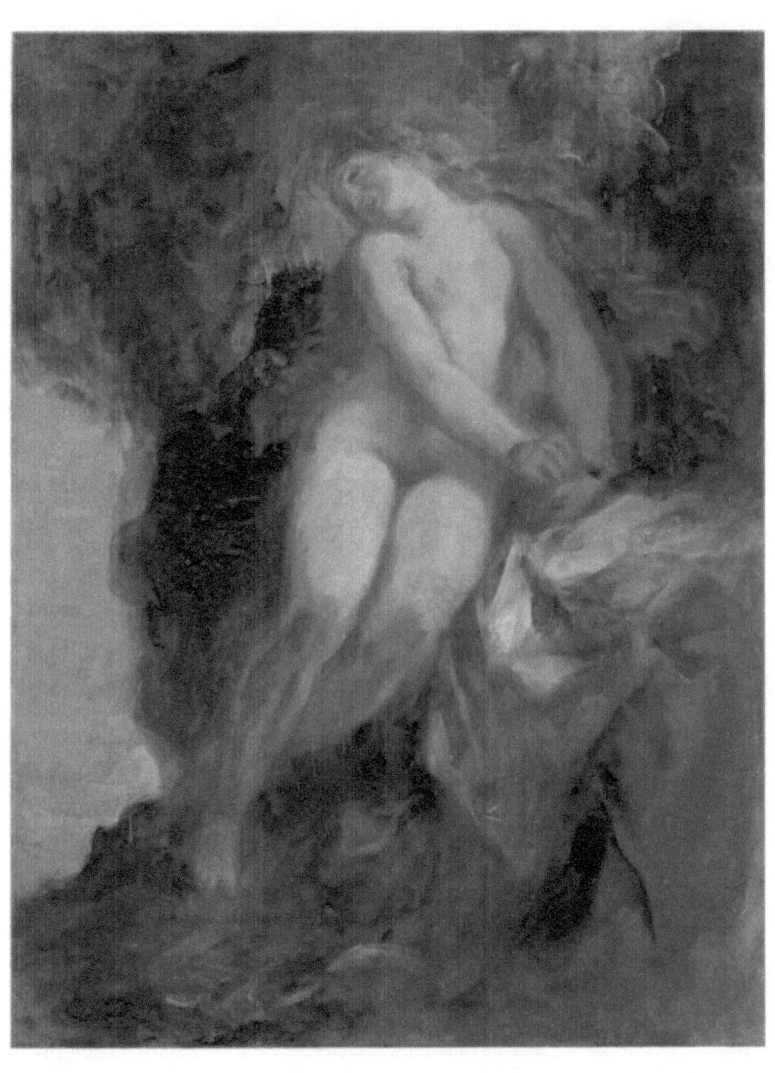

Andromeda, c.1852
Oil on canvas

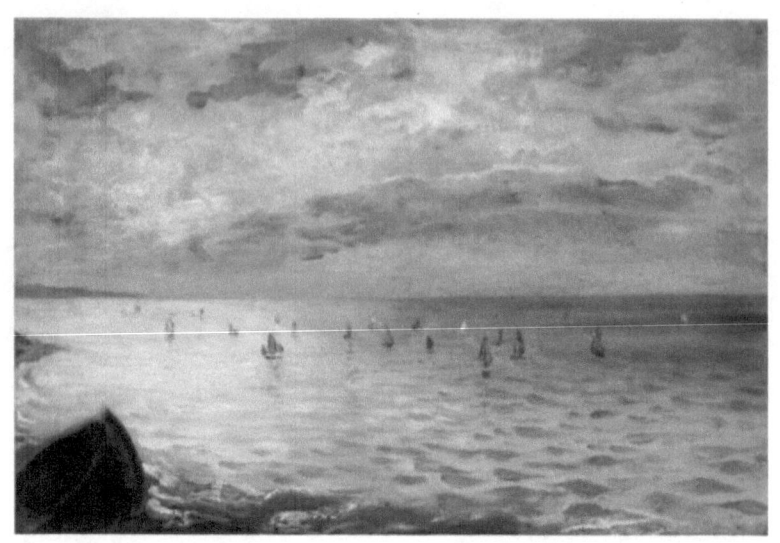

Sea Viewed from the Heights of Dieppe , 1852
Oil on canvas

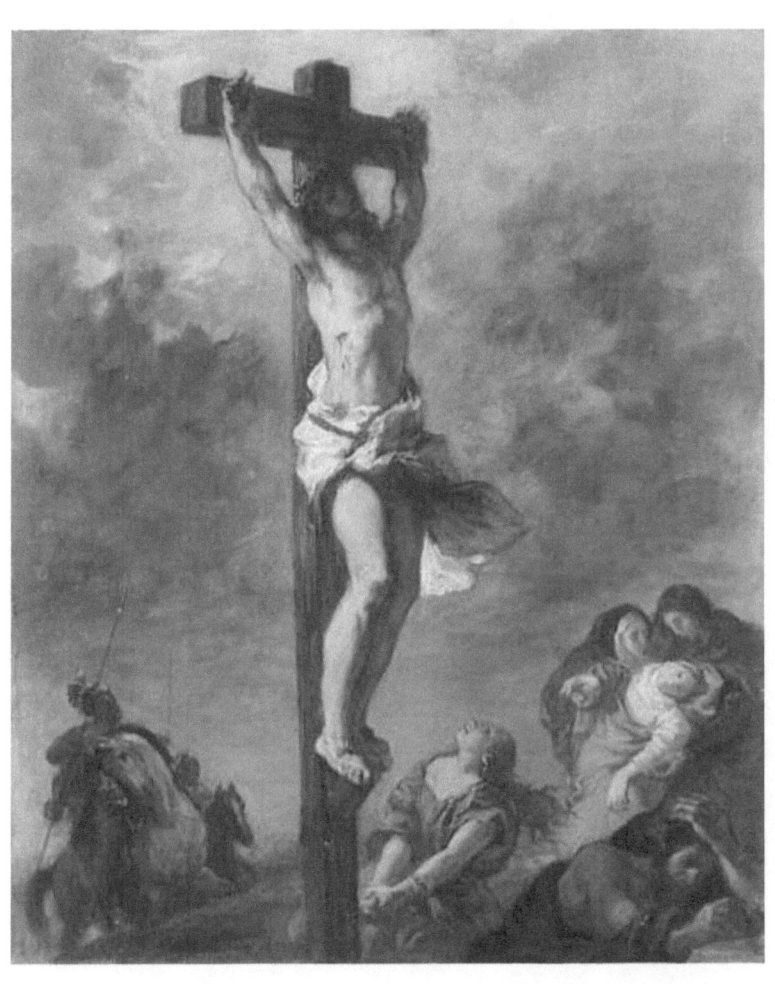

Christ on the Cross, 1853
Oil

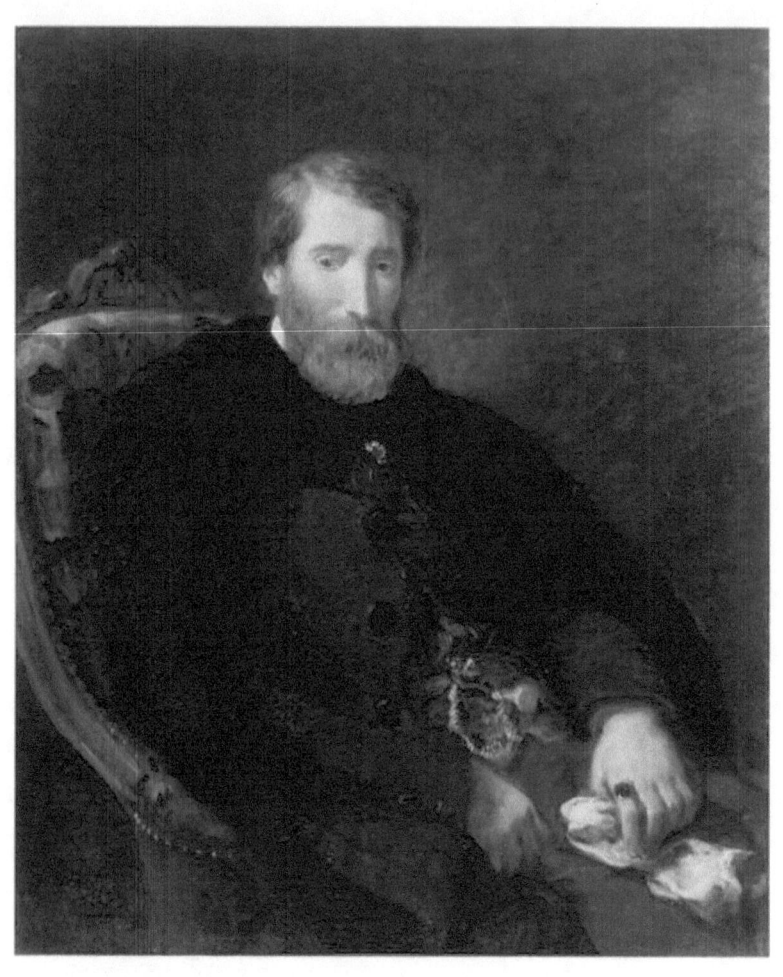

Portrait of Alfred Bruyas , 1853
Oil on canvas

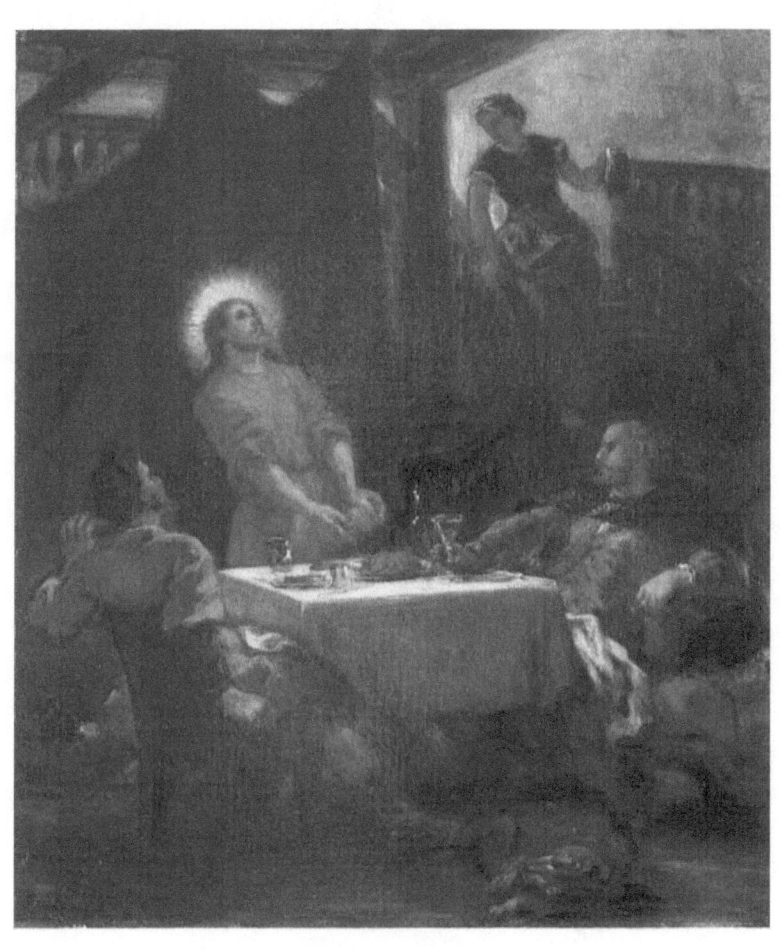

The Disciples at Emmaus, 1853
Oil on canvas

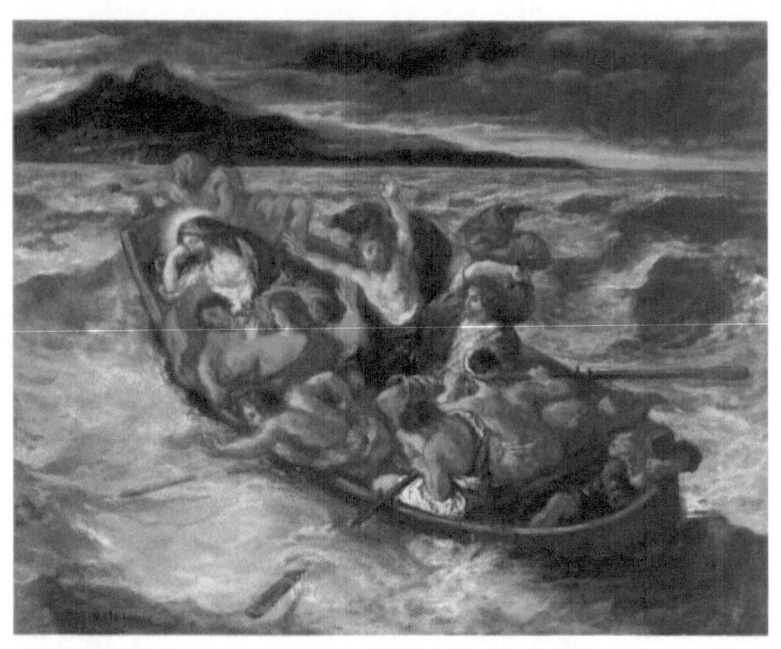

Christ on the Lake of Gennezaret, 1854
Oil on canvas

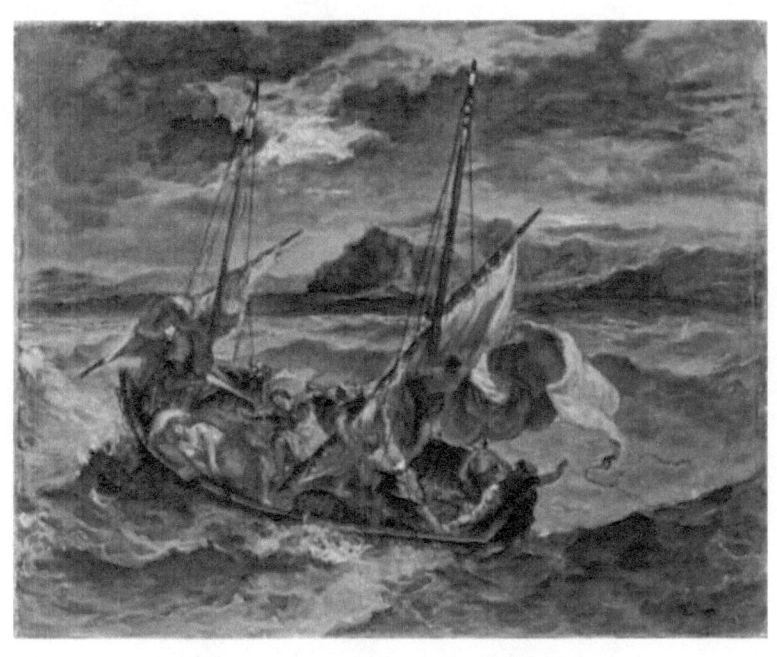

Christ on the Sea of Galilee, 1854
Oil on canvas

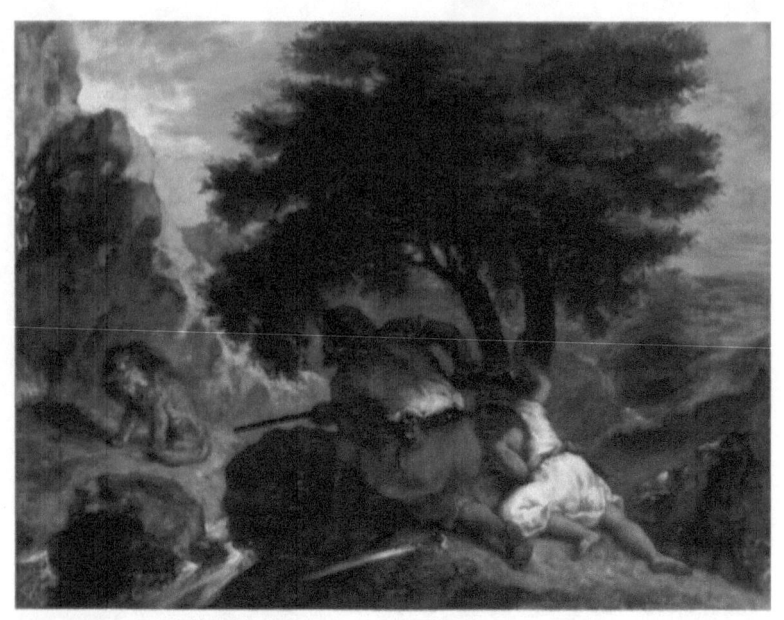

Lion Hunt in Morocco, 1854
Oil on canvas

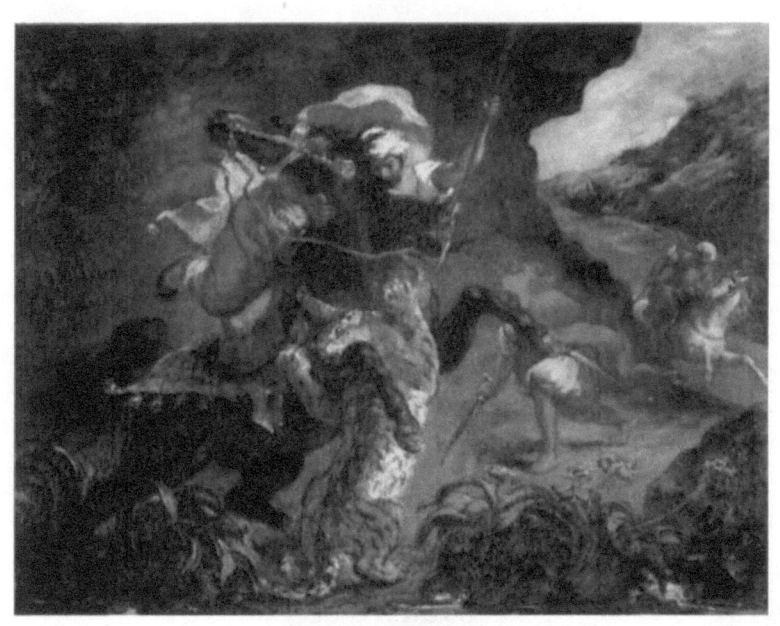

Tiger Hunt, 1854
Oil on canvas

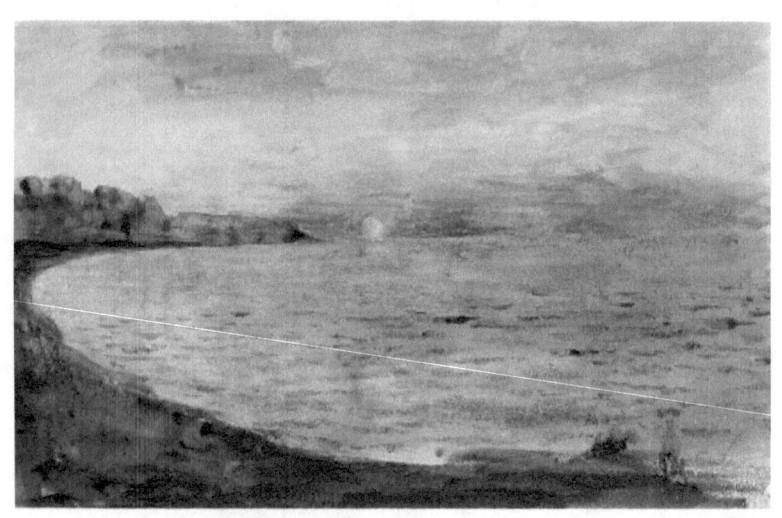

Cliffs near Dieppe, 1855
Watercolor

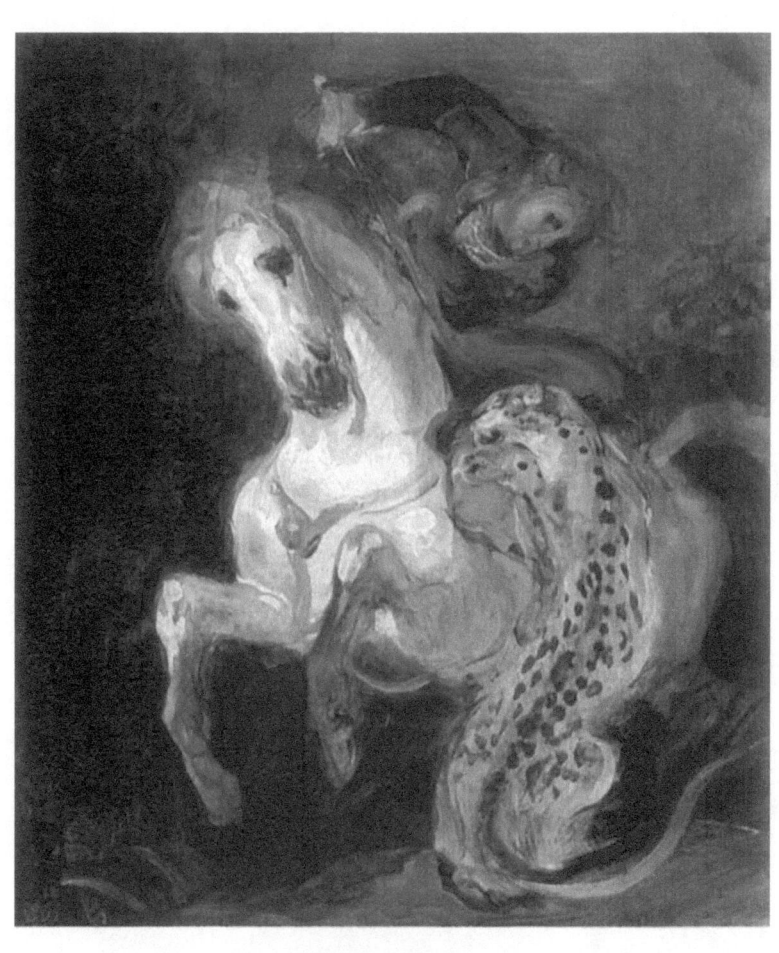

Jaguar Attacking a Horseman, c. 1855
Oil on canvas

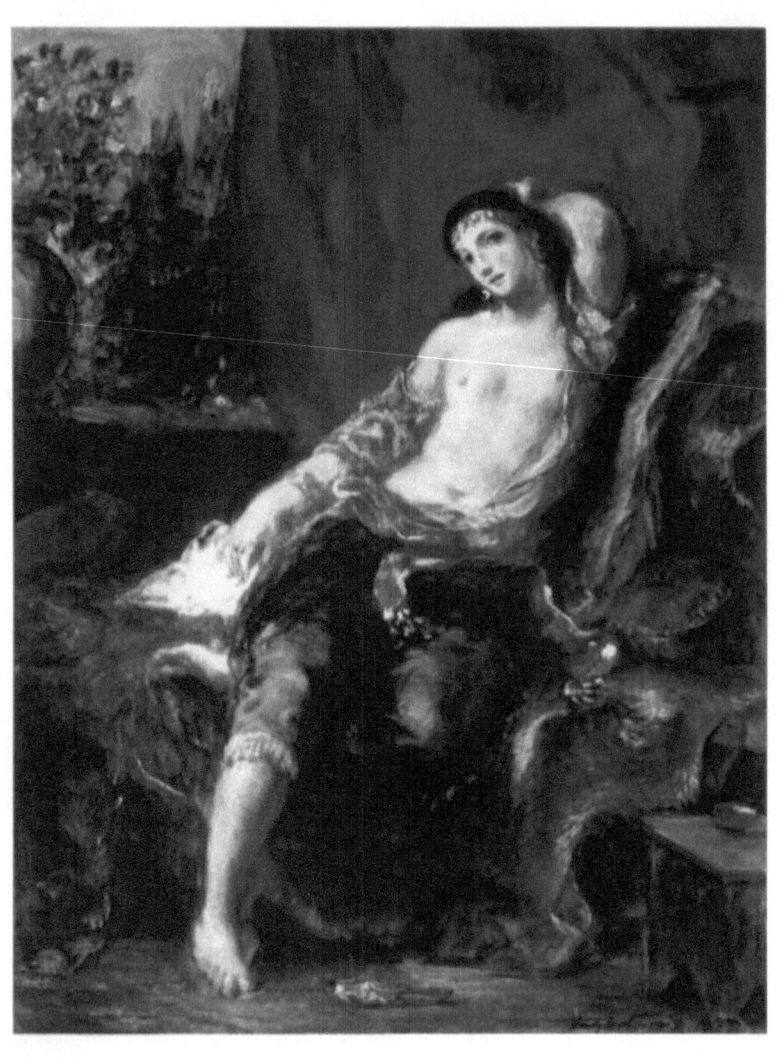

Odalisque, 1857
Oil on wood

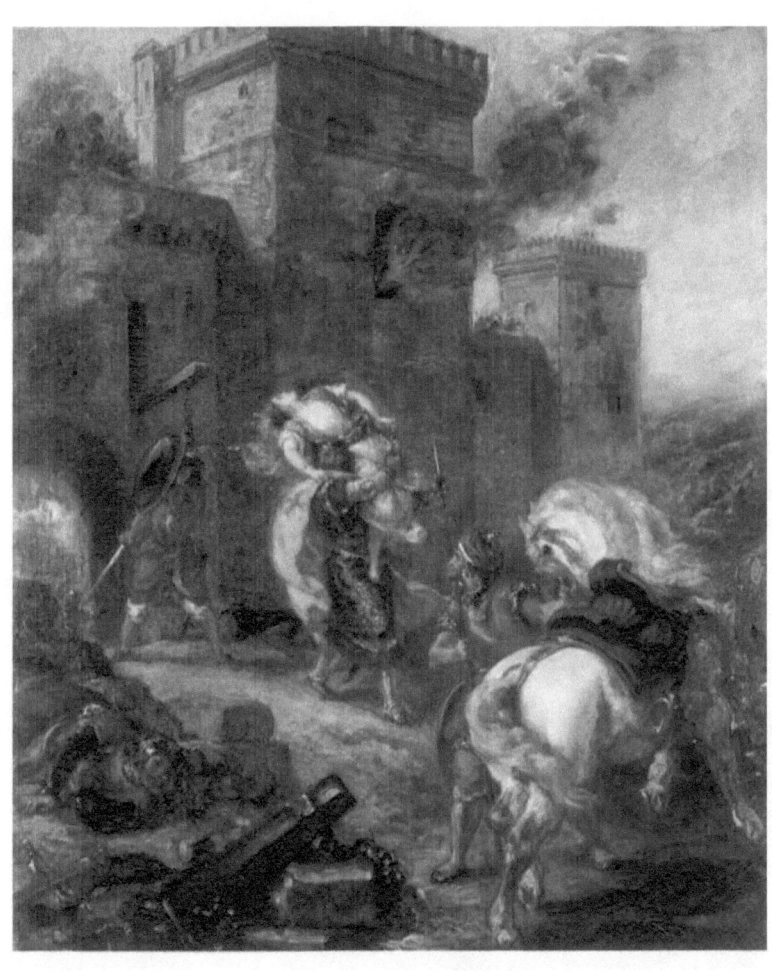

Rebecca Kidnapped by the Templar, Sir Brian de Bois-
Guilbert, 1858
Oil on canvas

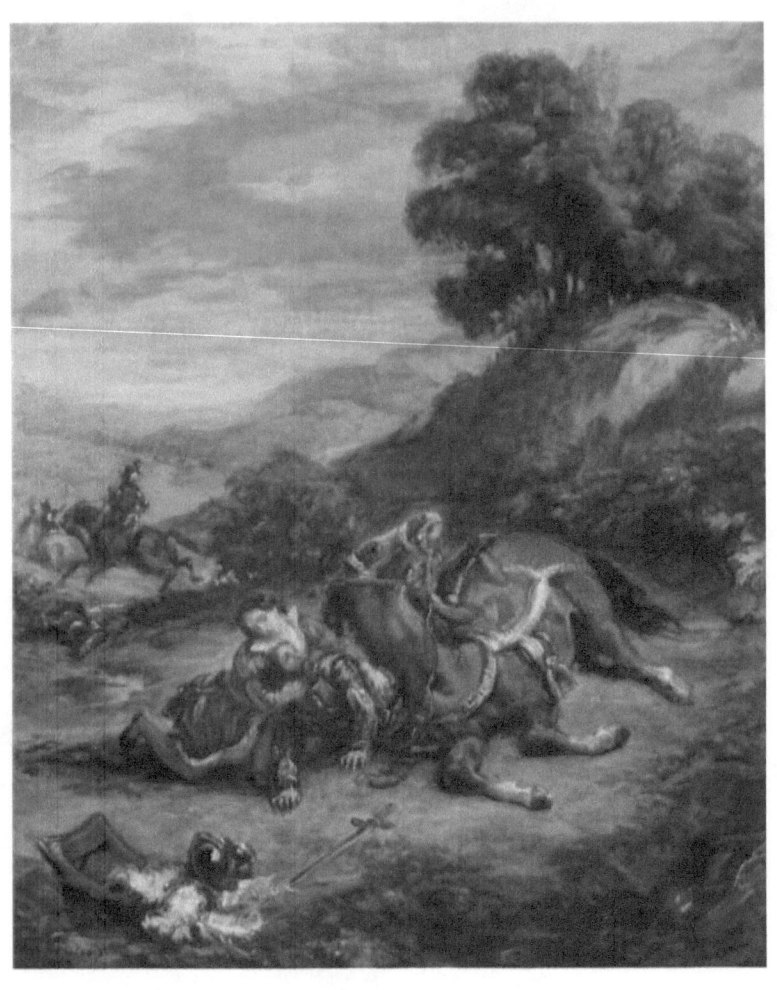

The death of Laras, 1858
Oil on canvas

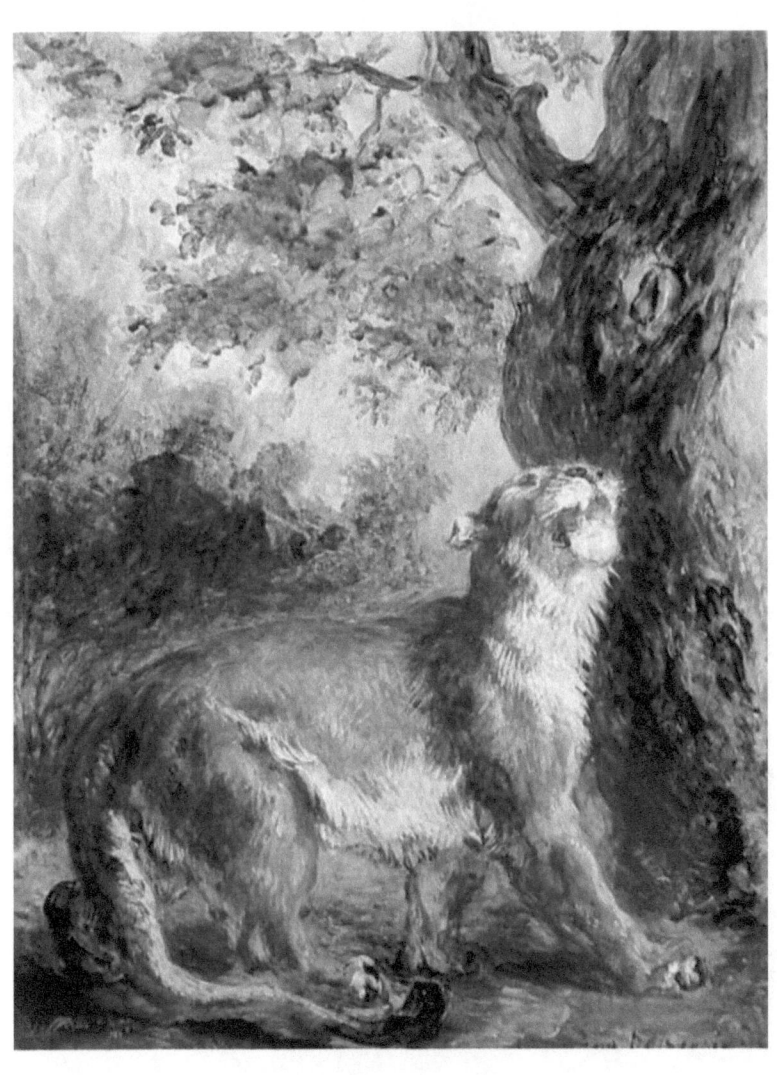

Puma (Lioness watching prey), 1859
Oil on canvas

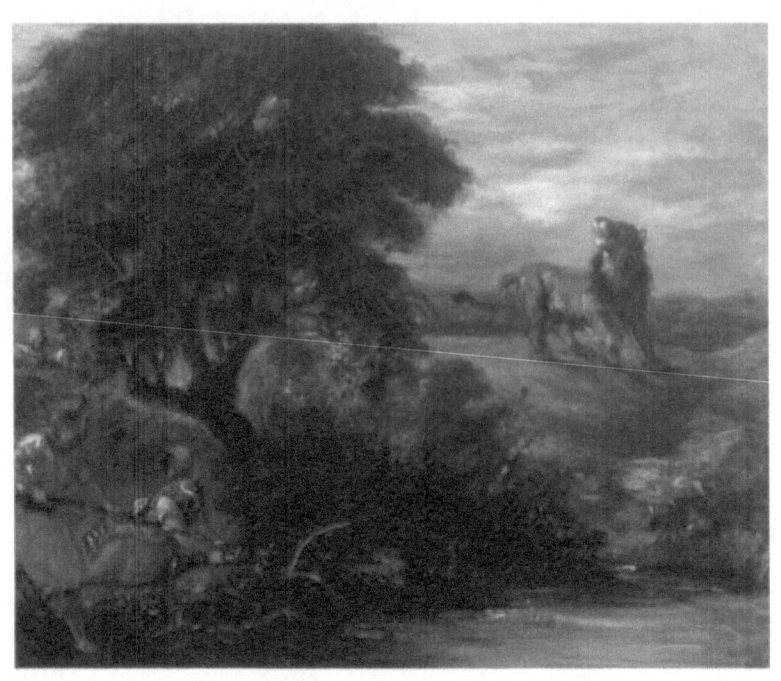

The Lion Hunt, 1859
Oil on canvas

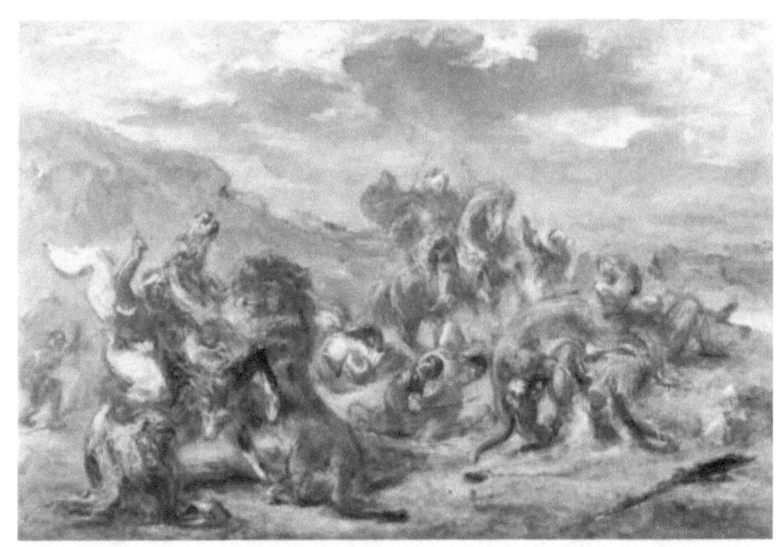

Lion Hunt, c.1860
Oil on canvas

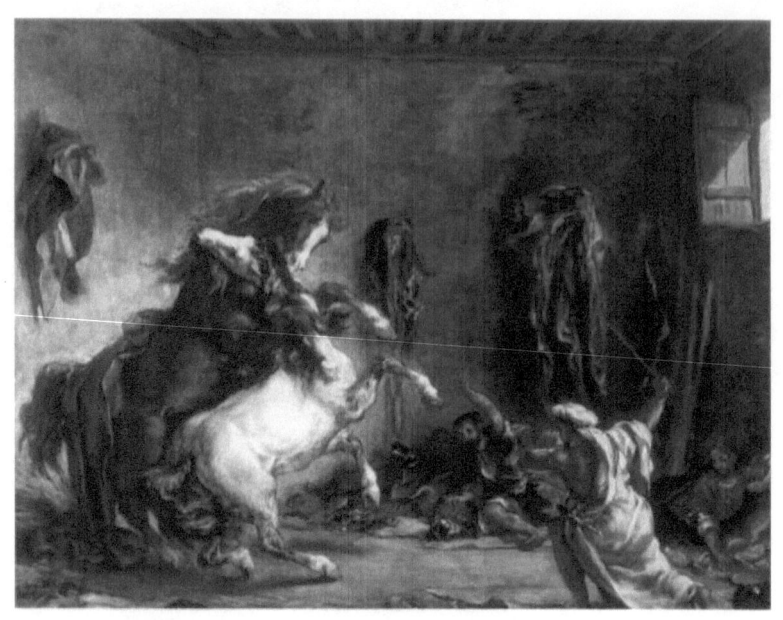

Arab Horses Fighting in a Stable, 1860
Oil on canvas

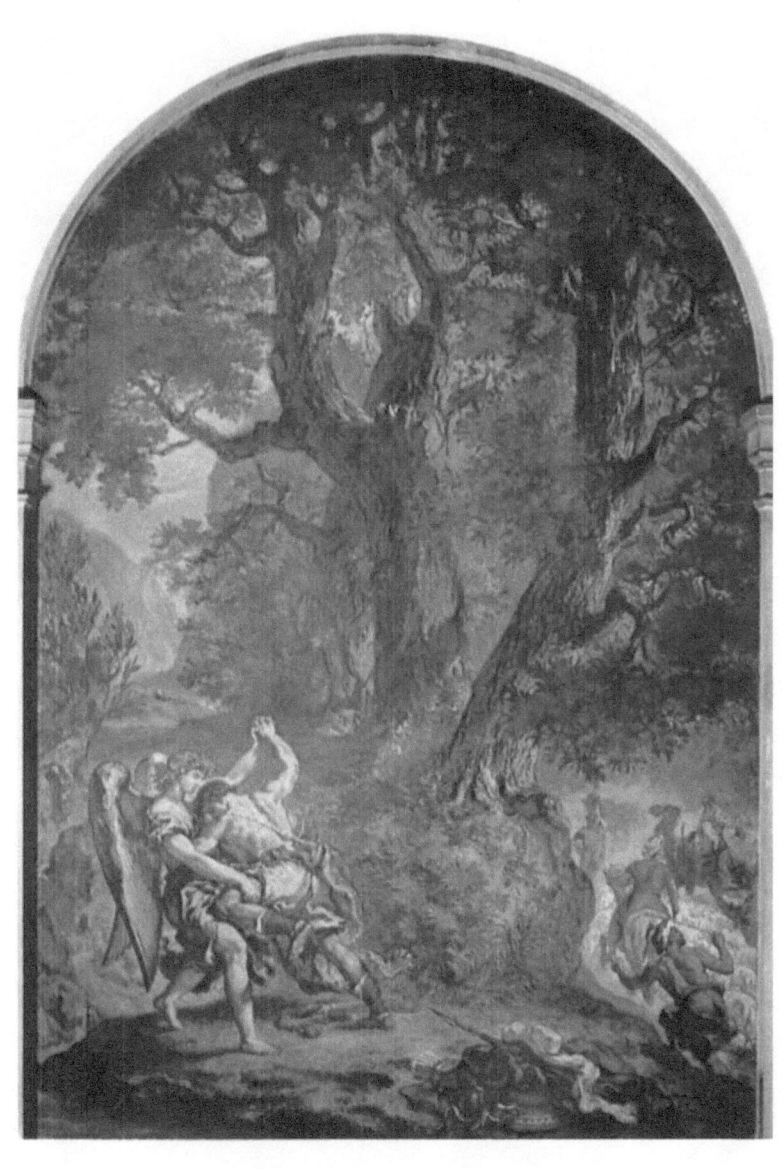

Jacob's fight with the angel, 1856-1861
Oil on canvas

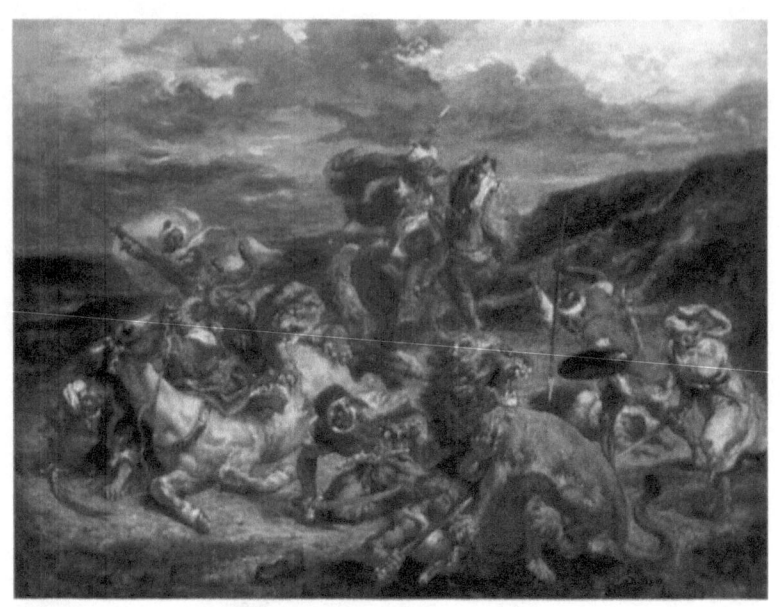

Lion Hunt, 1861
Oil on canvas

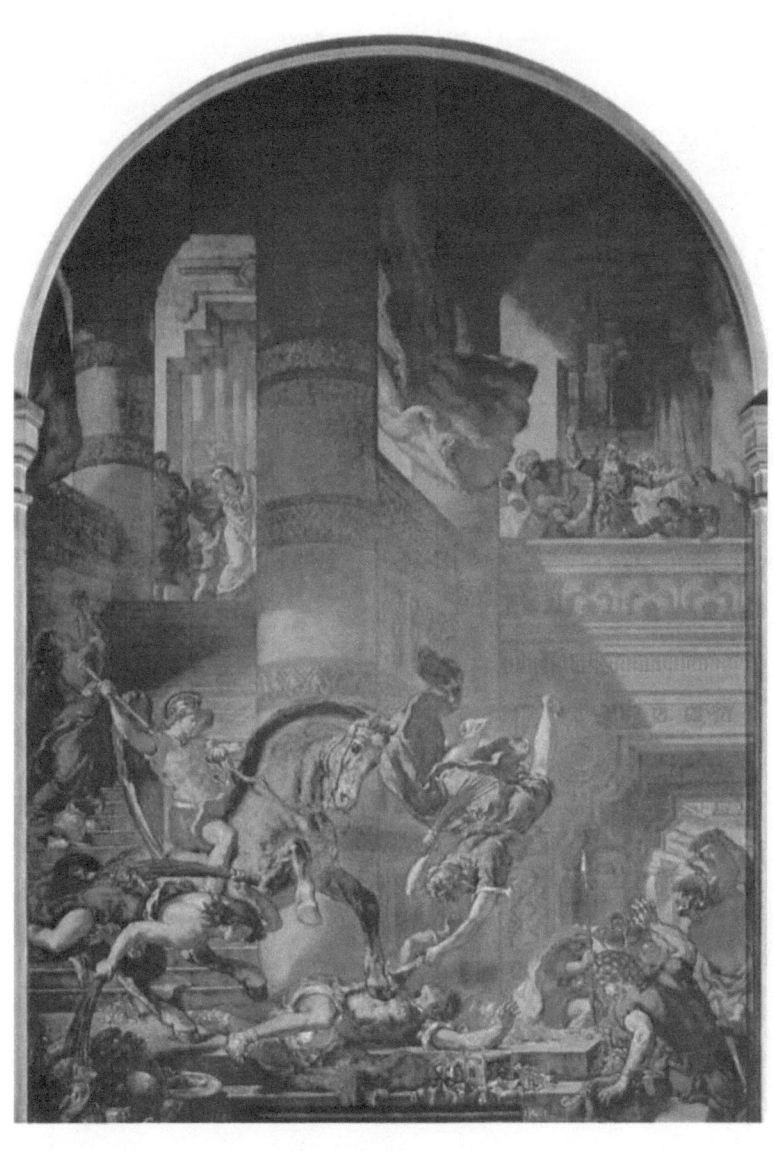

The Expulsion of Heliodorus, 1856-1861
Oil on canvas

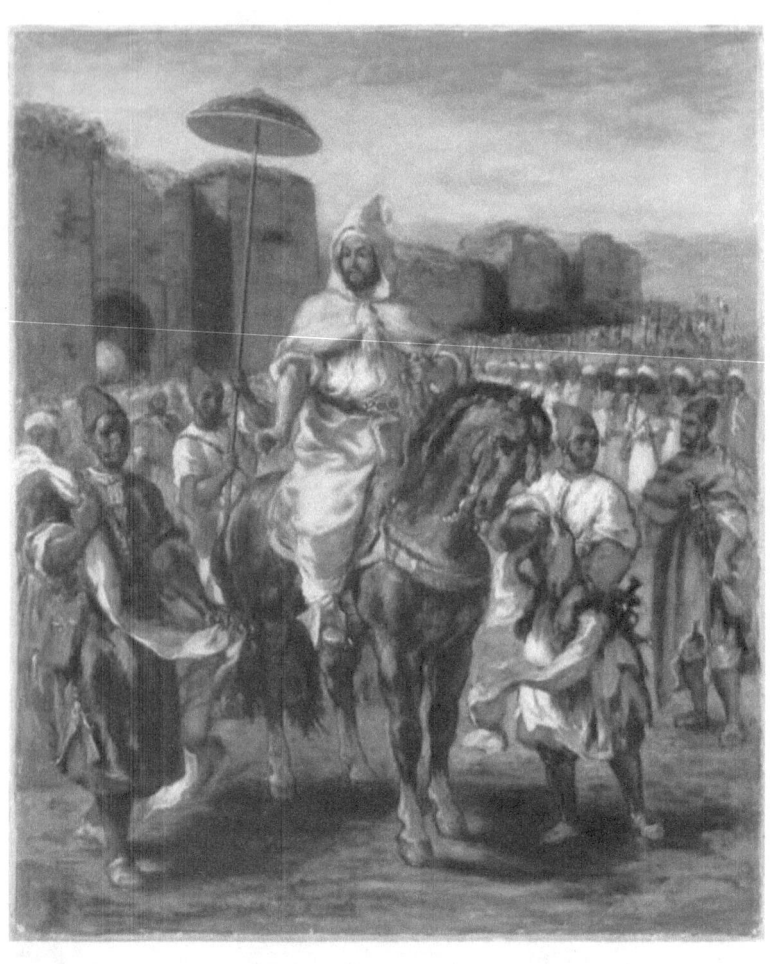

Portrait of the Sultan of Morocco, 1862
Oil on canvas

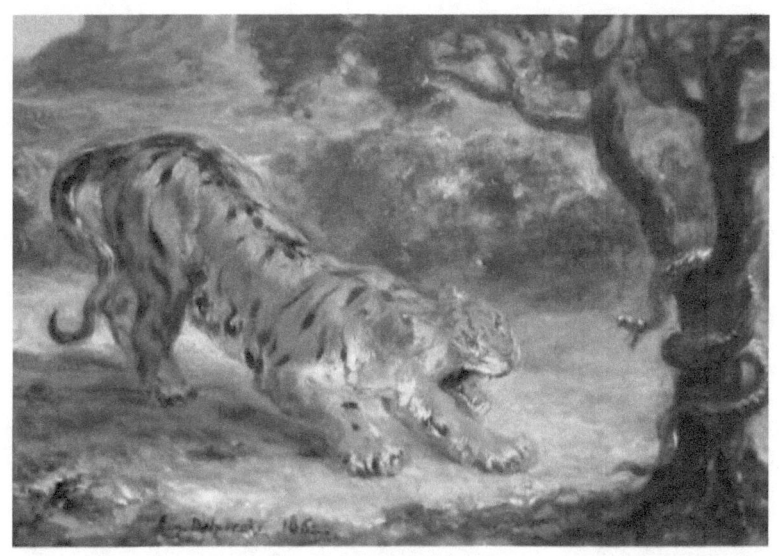

Tiger and Snake, 1862
Oil on canvas

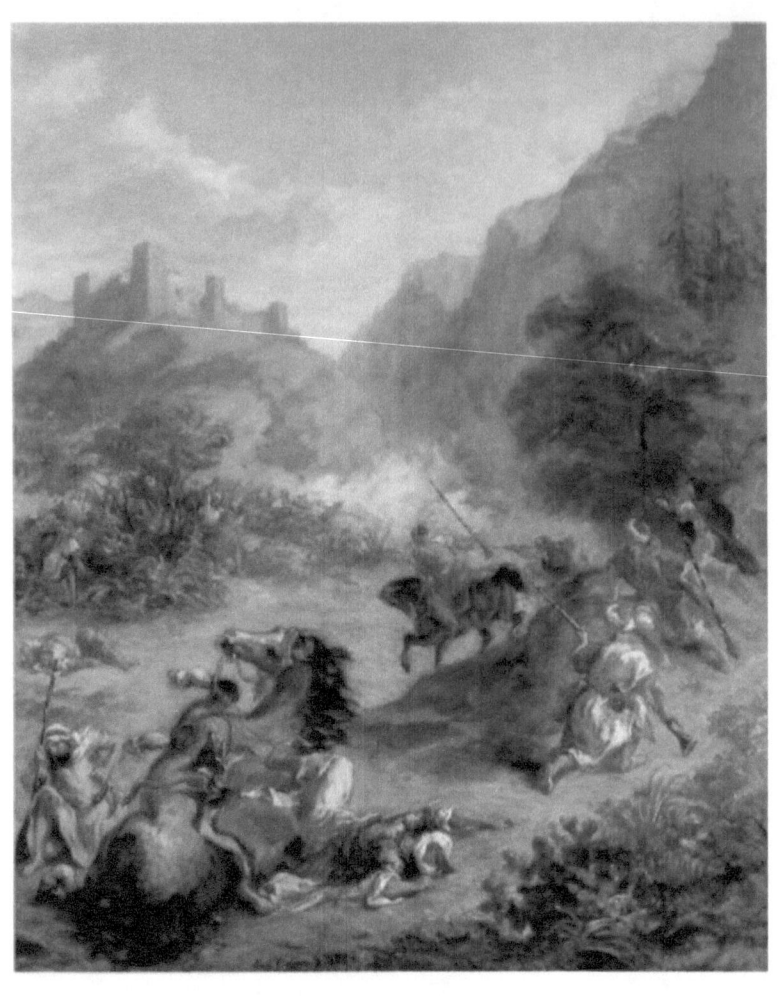

Arabs Skirmishing in the Mountains, 1863
Oil on canvas

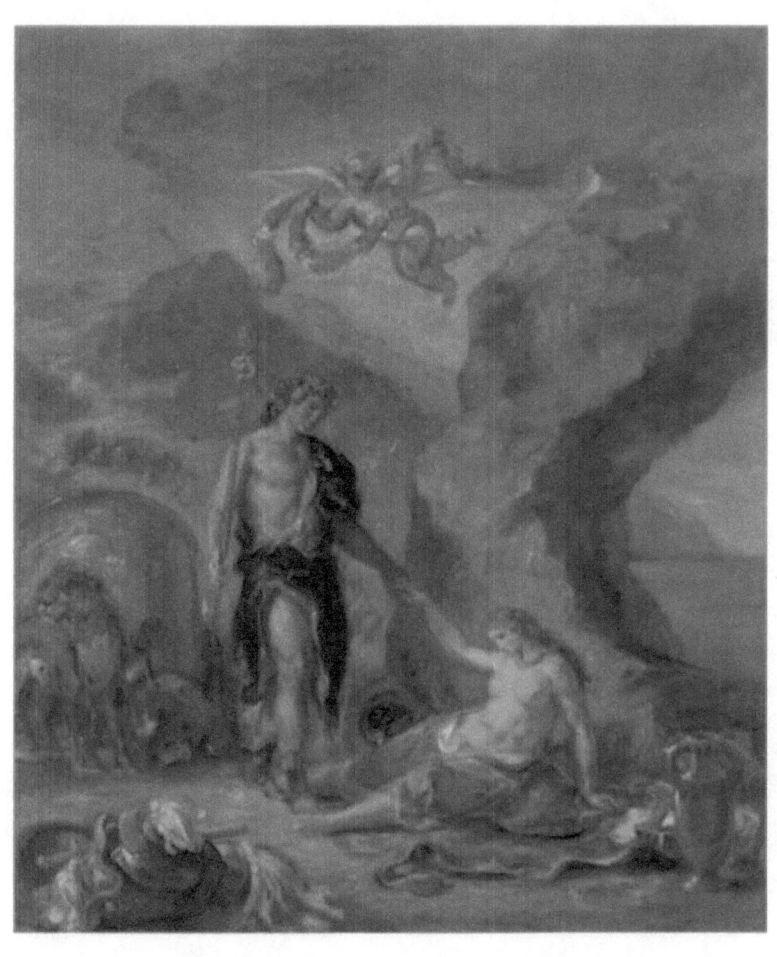

The Autumn Bacchus and Ariadne, 1856-1863
Oil on canvas

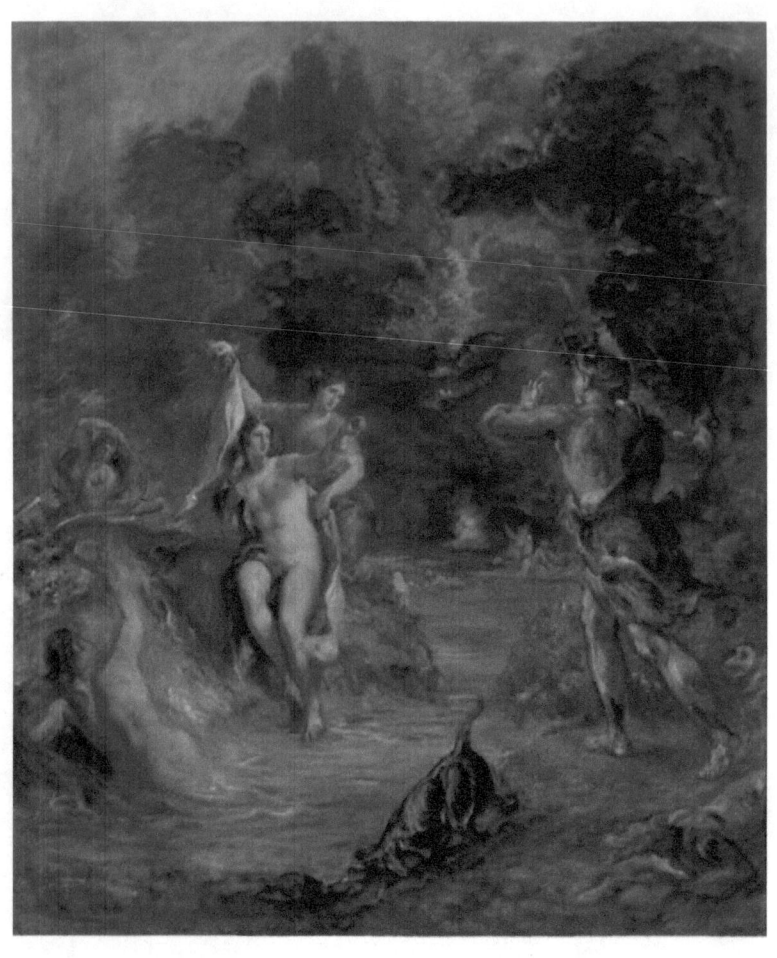

The Summer Diana Surprised by Actaeon, 1856-1863
Oil on canvas

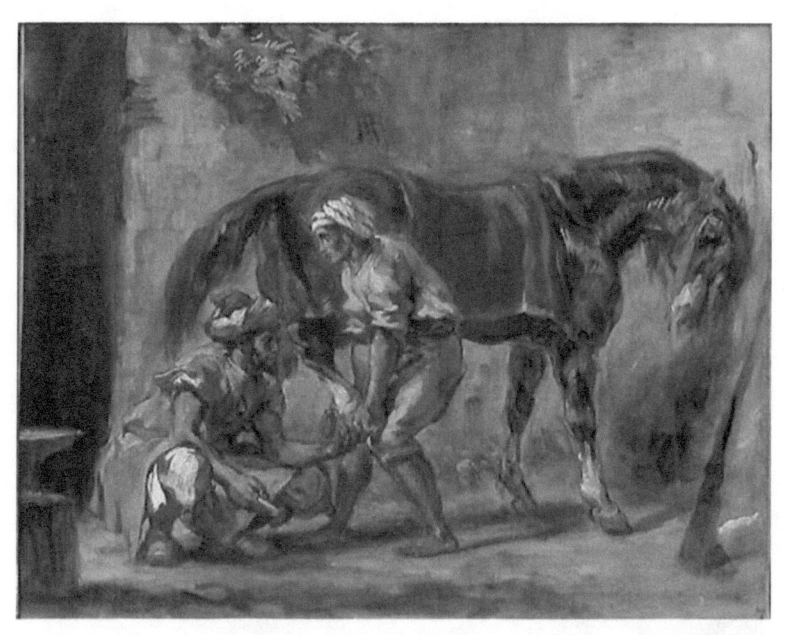

A blacksmith
Oil on canvas

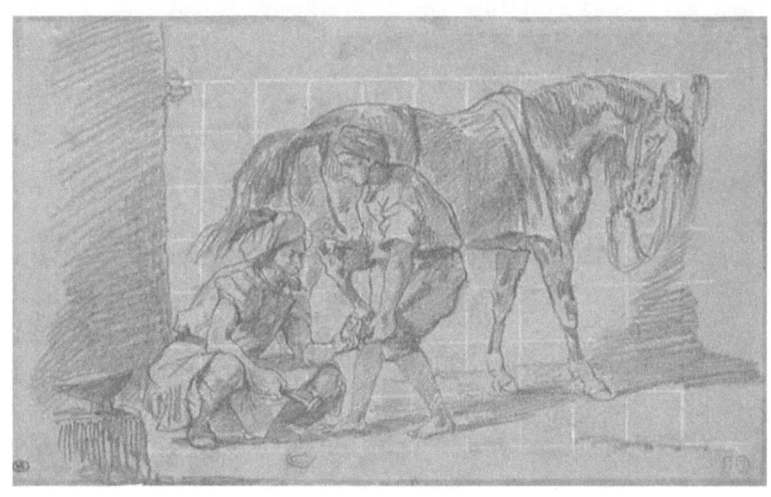

A blacksmith
Chalk

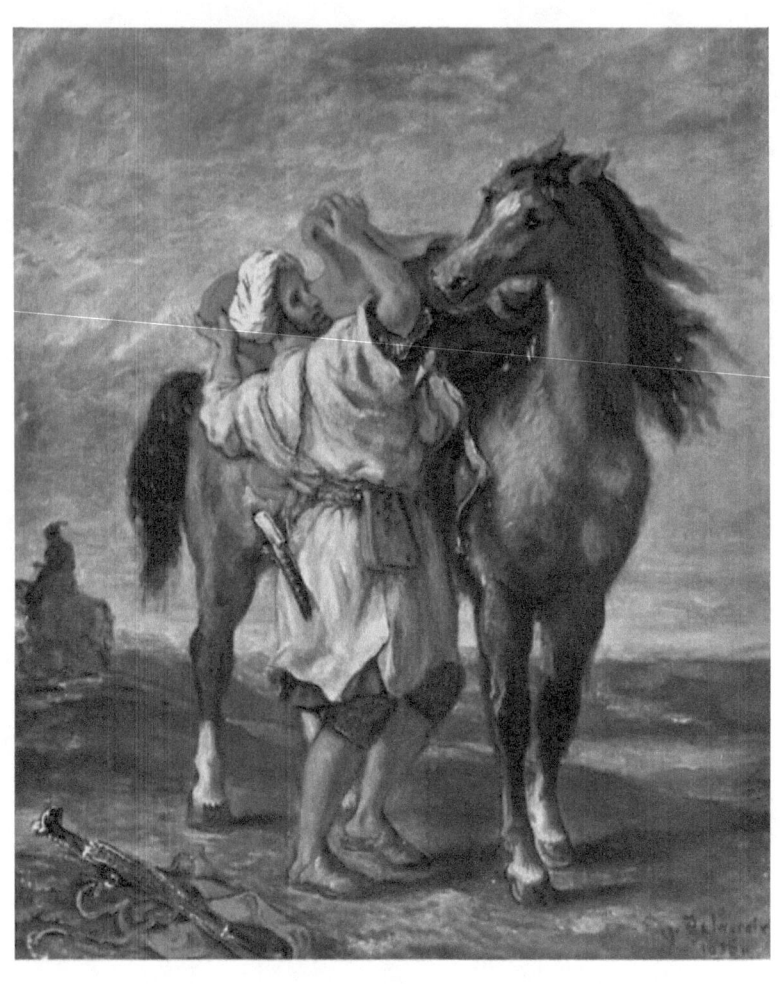

A Moroccan Saddling a Horse
Oil on canvas

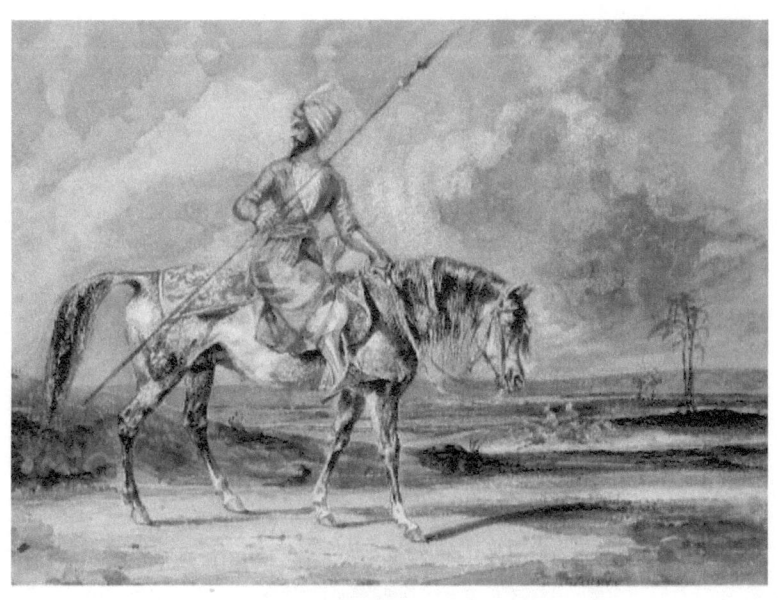

A Turkish Man on a Grey Horse
Watercolor

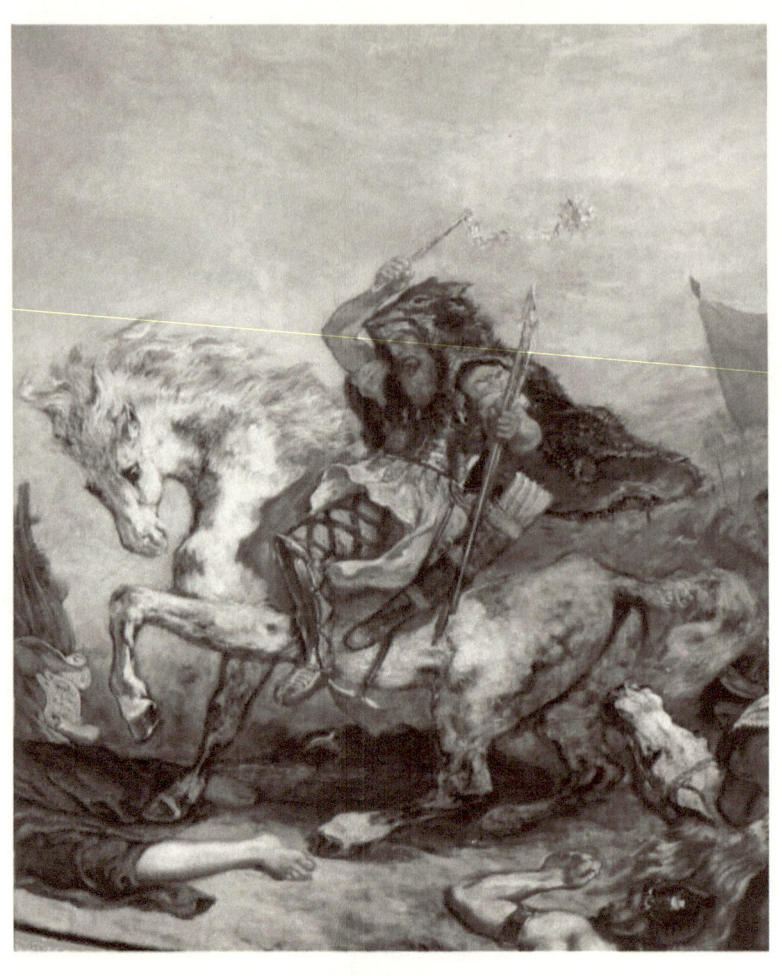

Attila the Hun
Oil on canvas

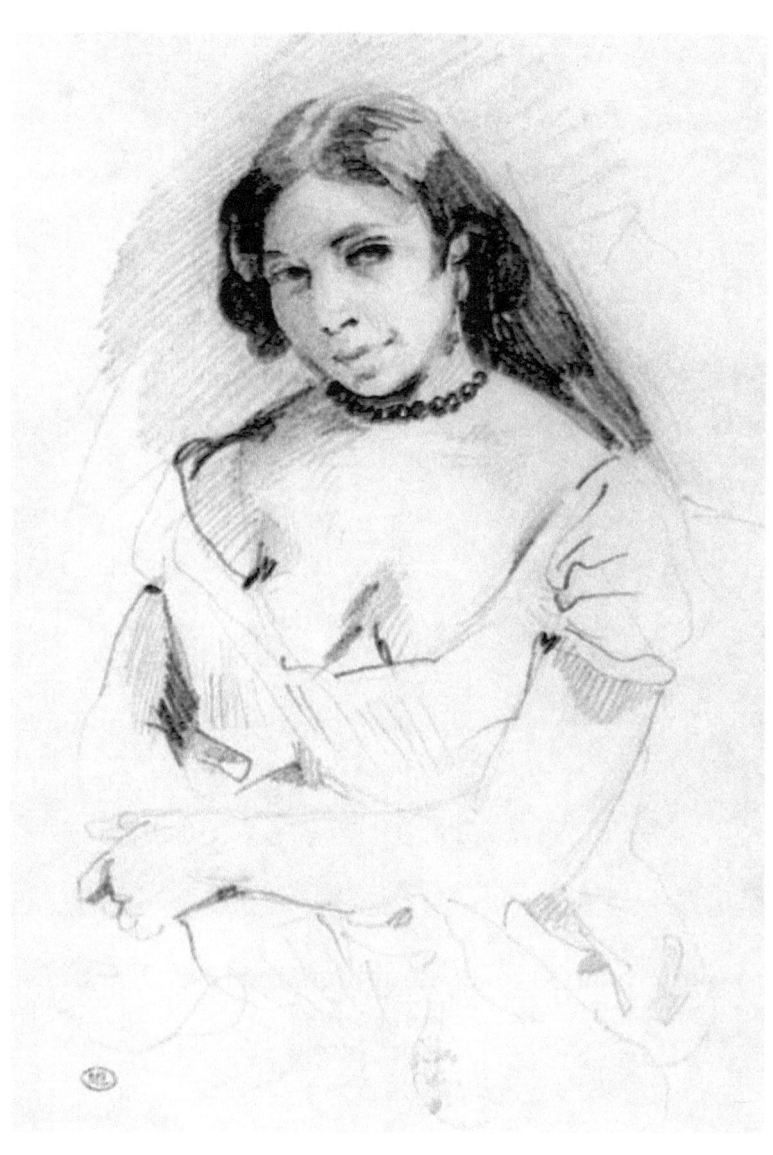

Aspasia

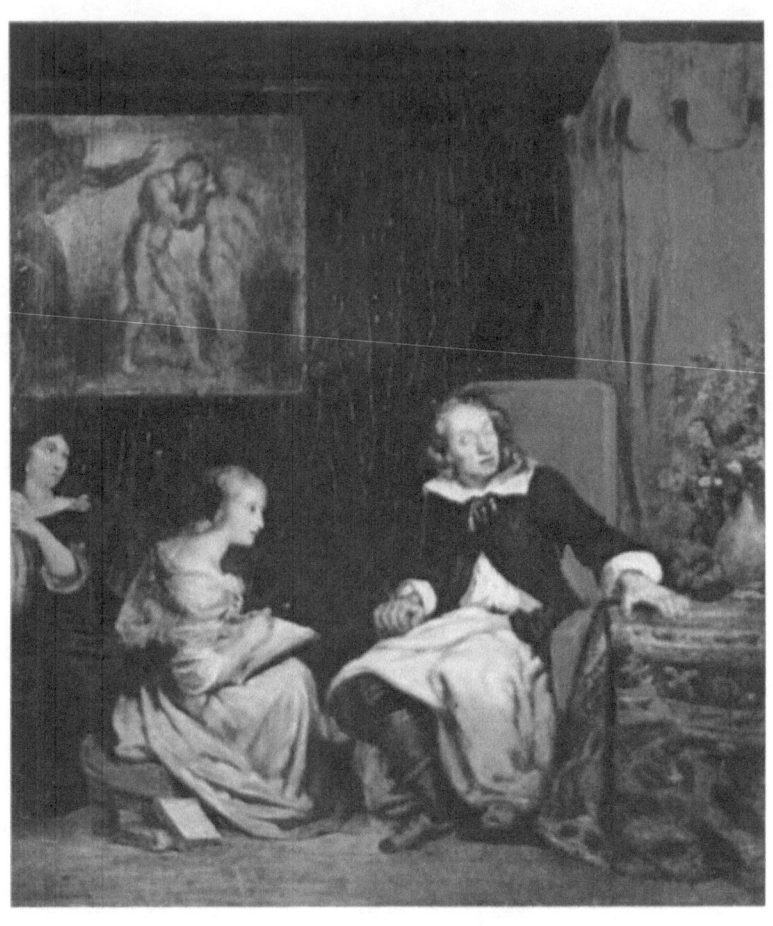

Milton dictated to his daughters the (Paradise Lost)
Oil on canvas

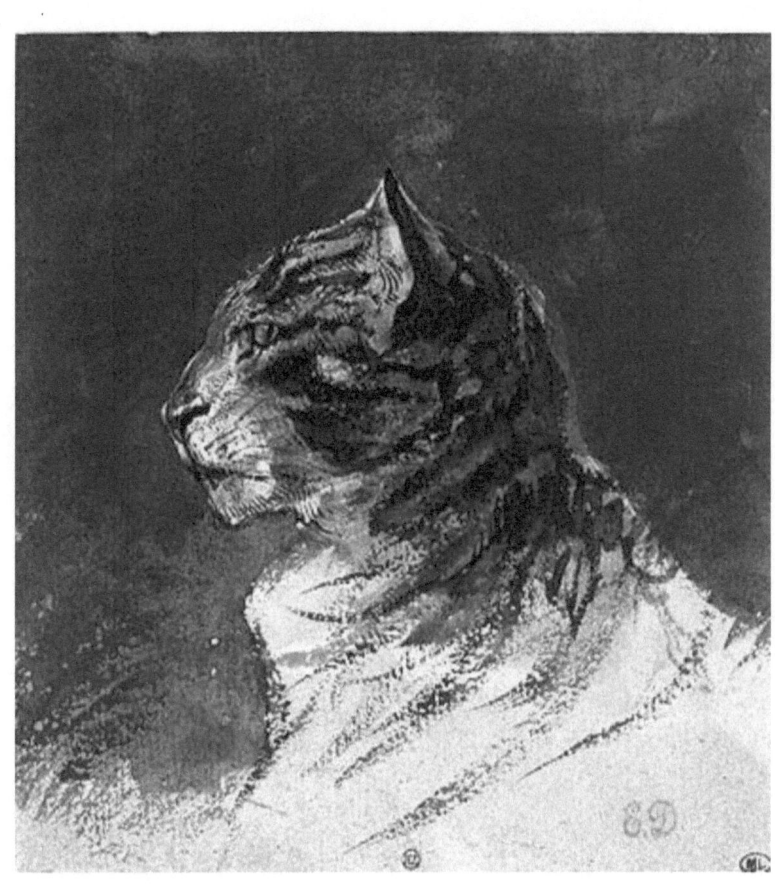

Cat head

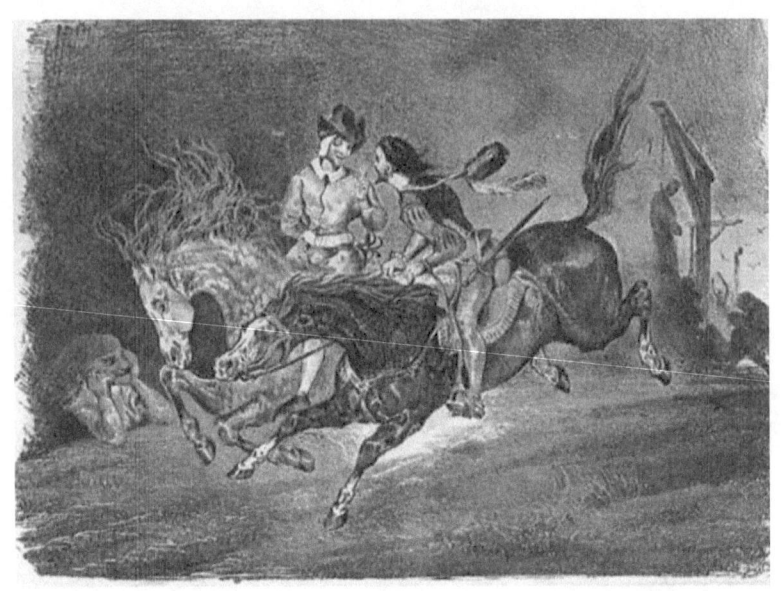

Faust

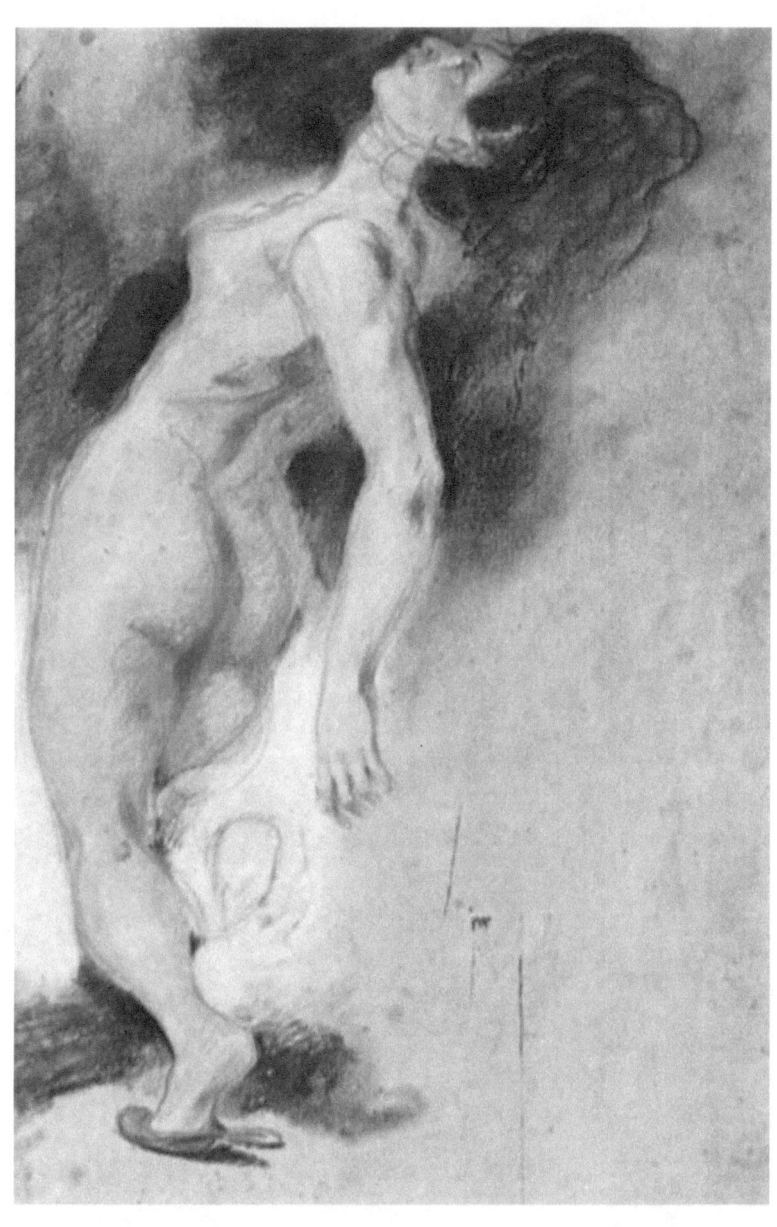

Female Nude Killed from Behind
Pastel

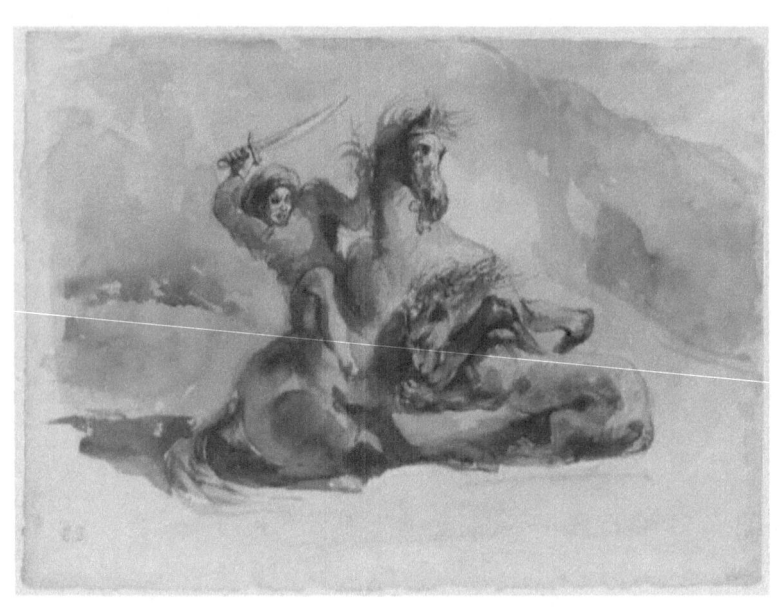

Horse and Rider Attacked by a Lion
Watercolor

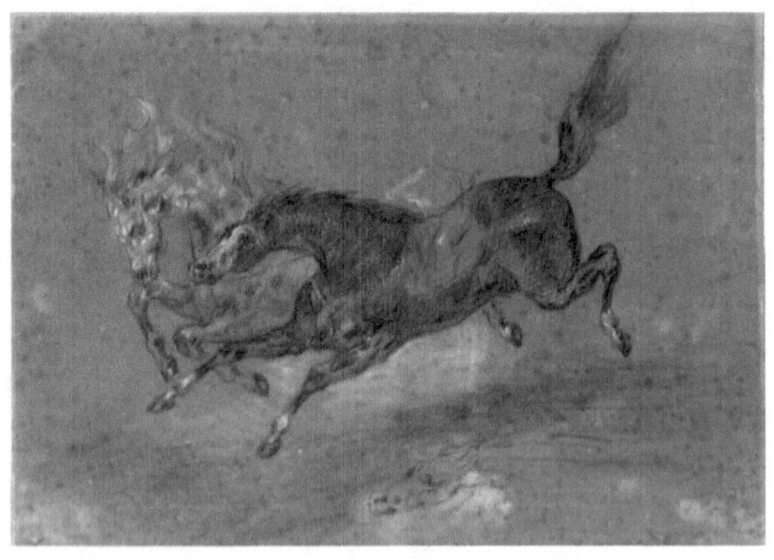

Horses running

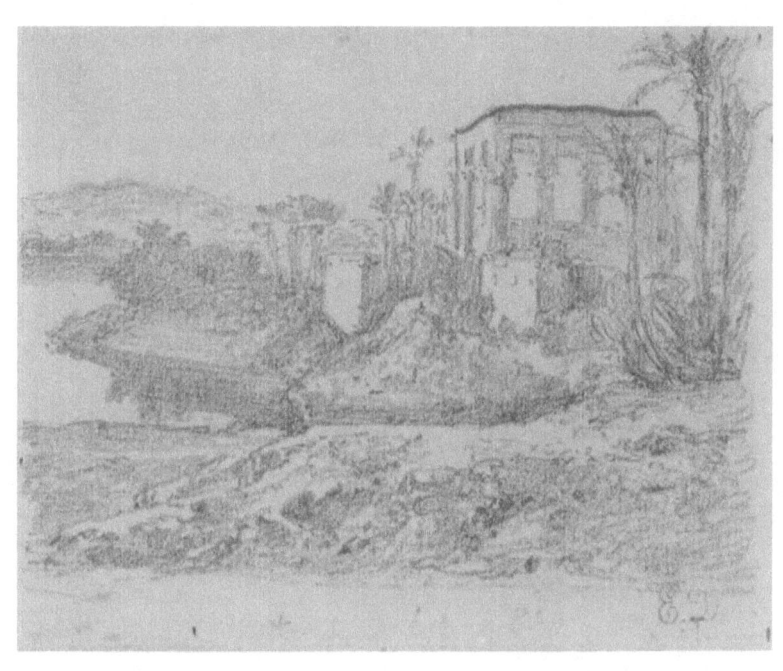

Kiosk of Trajan at Philae

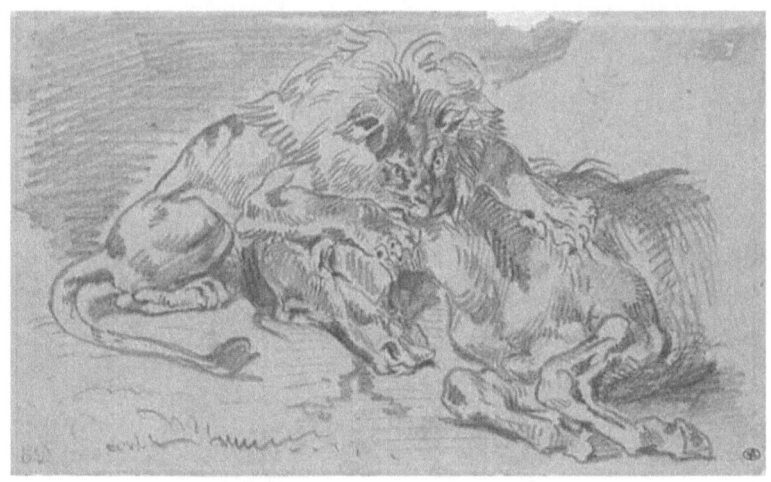

Lion Devouring a Horse

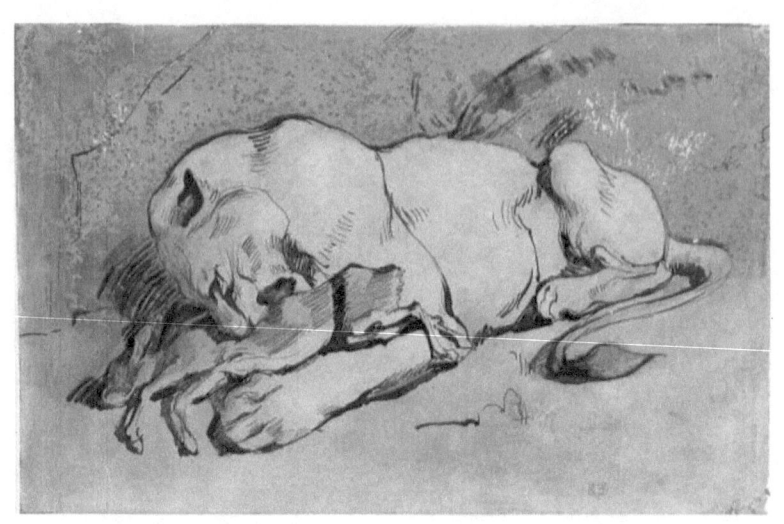

Lioness devouring a Rabbit
Pen

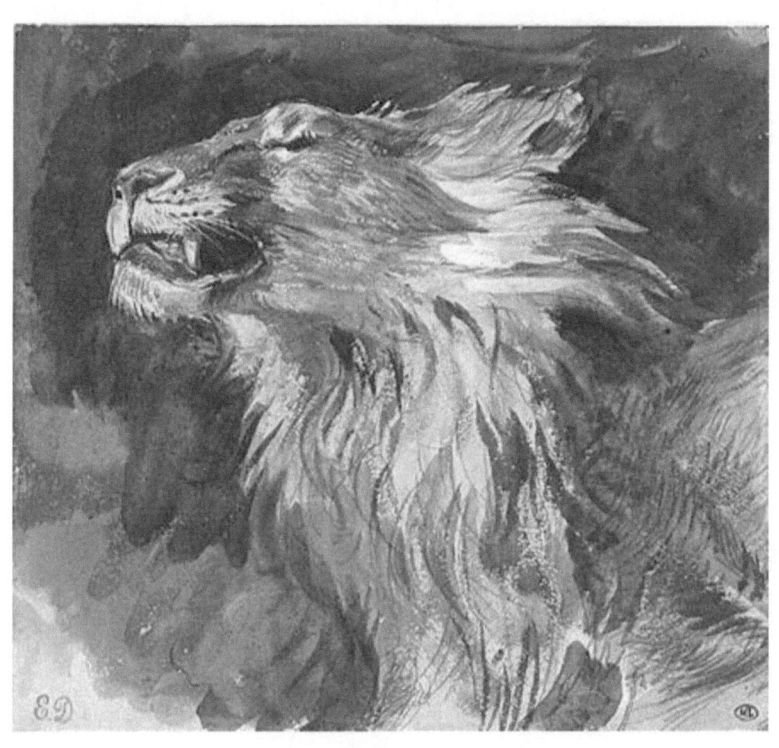

Roaring lion's head

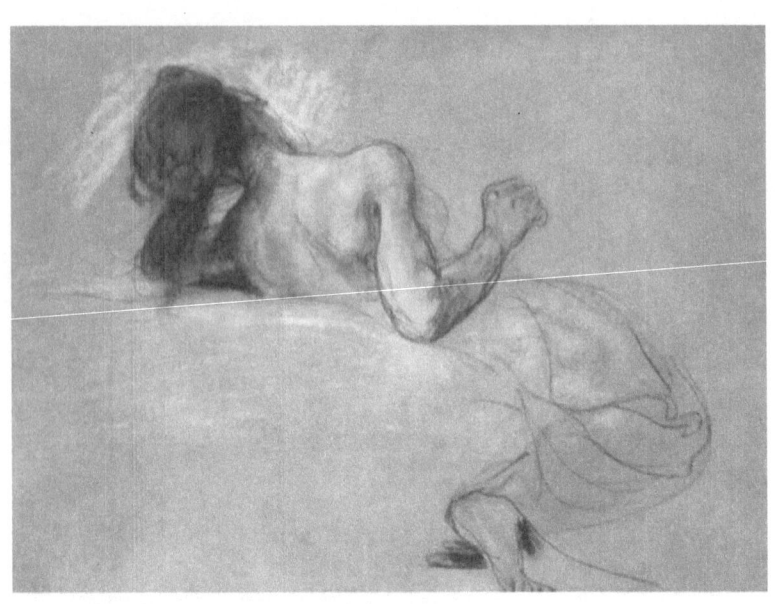

Study Sardanapalus

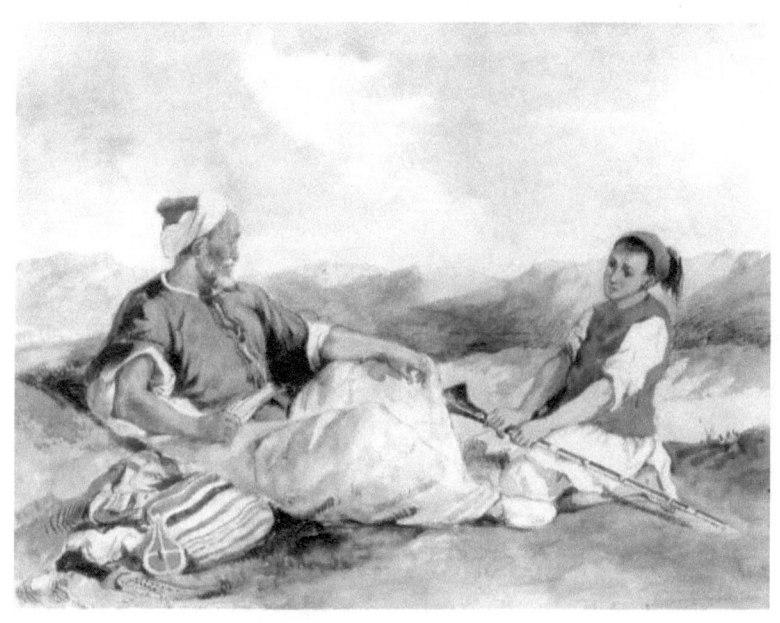

Two Moroccans Seated in the Countryside
Watercolor

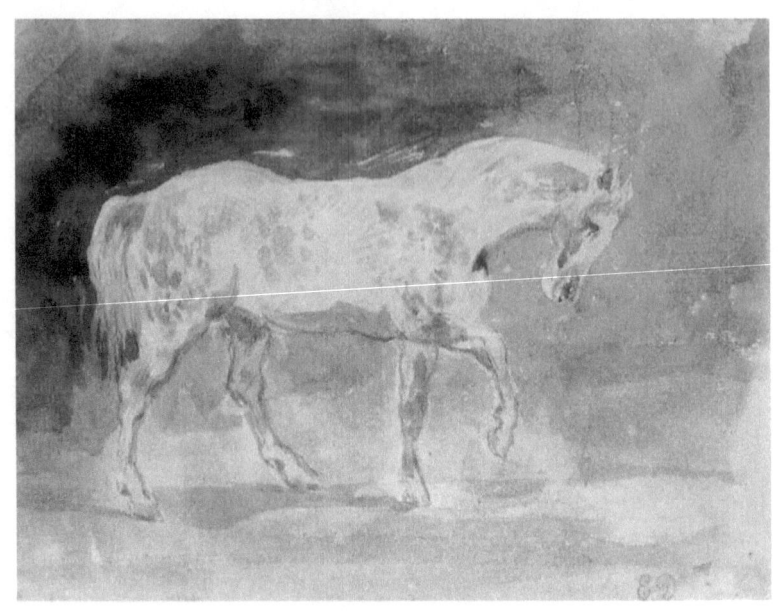

Horse
Watercolor

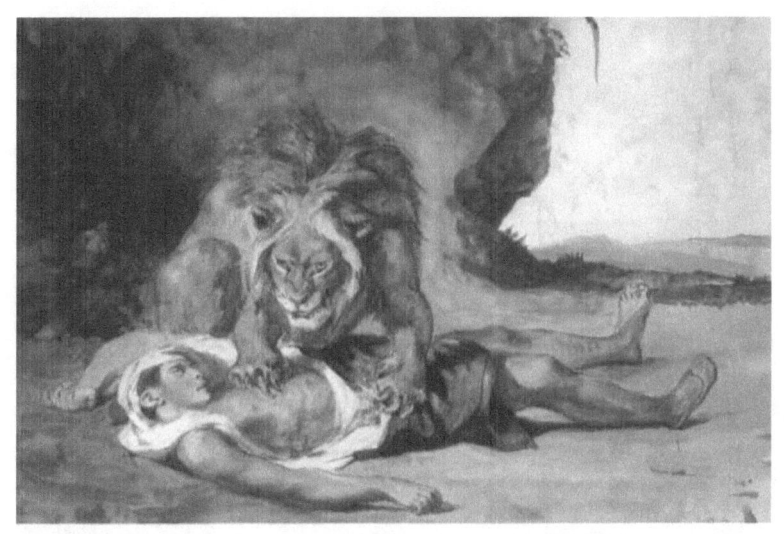

Lion Rending Apart a Corpse
Watercolor

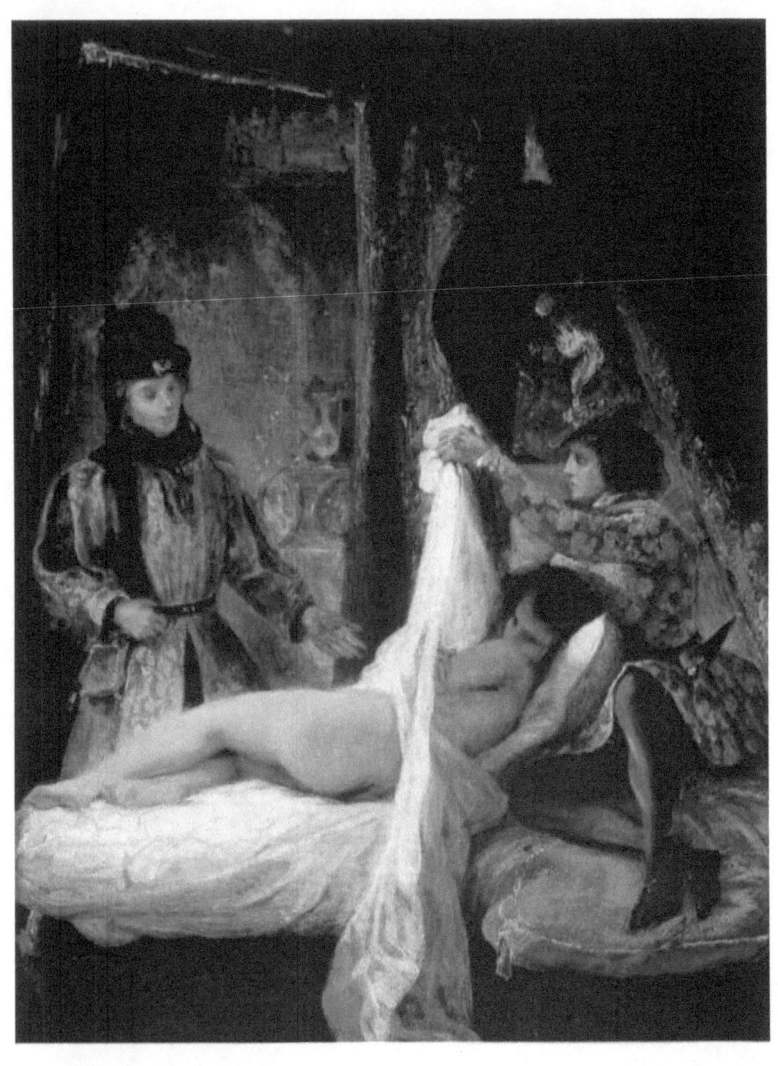

The Duc d'Orleans showing his Mistress to the Duc de
Bourgogne
Oil on canvas

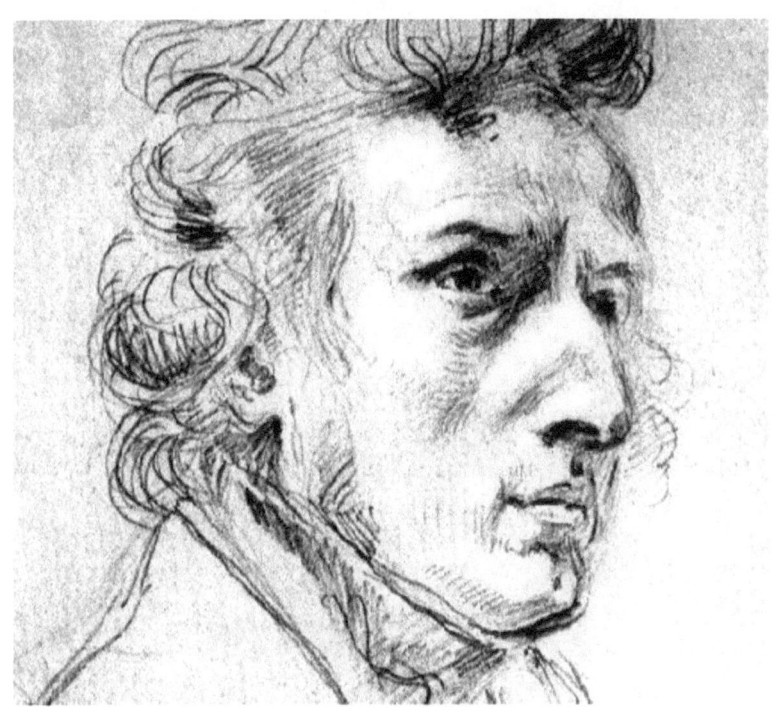

Chopin